D0881710

Spirit Wind

The
Ultimate Adventure

Dr. Dale A. Fife

Unless otherwise indicated, all Scripture quotations are taken from the *Holy Bible*, New King James Version, copyright © 1979, 1980, 1982. Used by permission of Thomas Nelson, Inc., Nashville, Tennessee.

Scripture quotations marked KJV are taken from the *Holy Bible*, King James Authorized Version, which is in the public domain. Scripture quotations marked MSG are taken from *The Message*, copyright © by Eugene H. Peterson. Published by Nav Press, Colorado Springs, Colorado, in association with Alive Communications, Colorado Springs, Colorado.

Spirit Wind: The Ultimate Adventure

ISBN: 0-924748-68-0
UPC: 88571300038-3

Printed in the United States of America
© 2006 by Dr. Dale \A. Fife

Milestones International Publishers
140 Danika Dr., NW
Huntsville, AL 35806
Phone: 256-830-0362
        303-503-7257
FAX: 256-830-9206
E-mail: milestonesintl@bellsouth.net
www.milestonesintl.com

No part of this book may be reproduced or transmitted in any form or by any means, electronic or mechanical, including photocopying, recording, or by any information storage and retrieval system, without permission in writing from the publisher.

The author has exercised the liberty to capitalize certain words and phrases in this volume for the purpose of emphasis.

1 2 3 4 5 6 7 8 9 10 11 / 09 08 07 06

ENDORSEMENTS

This book communicates on two levels. At the obvious level it imparts understanding into how God equips and prepares His end-time warriors. But don't stop there. As you join the author on his spiritual journey, your heart will be apprehended with longing to find *Spirit Wind* yourself and launch out on your own pilgrimage into the heart of God. It's time that we be awakened to the exhilarating potential of the secret place – the launch pad from which we discover all that the Spirit of truth would give us.

Bob Sorge

Speaker, teacher and author of many books including *Exploring Worship,*
The Fire of Delayed Answers and *Secrets of the Secret Place,* Oasis House

My friend and brother, Dale Fife, is a brilliant communicator of spiritual truth and spiritual reality. This book will break you out of any sense of routine and bring you into streams of refreshing and renewal in terms of direct experience with God. You'll discover once again, as if for the first time, how deep and abiding the love of Christ is for His sheep both found and lost.

Bishop Mark J. Chironna

From the Foreword

Spirit Wind is a launch venue for the heart of man to explore what could legitimately be called the realm of the spirit. As I read *Spirit Wind,* I was reminded that we are simply sojourners in this life and there really is a place of commanded blessing, where we are drawn into the presence of the Lord for great edification. Dr. Dale Arthur Fife invites us to take this journey and to realize that there really is a Kingdom that is beyond our mortal thinking. Prepare your heart for one of the most outstanding journeys of your lifetime. Like St. Paul's third heaven experience, you will be catapulted into places not seen by flesh and blood, but through the spiritual eyes only. Jesus is glorified and the soul is settled as we travel through time and space, coming into the beauty of His presence.

Dr. Fife once again invites us into the privacy of his own secret place journal and encourages all of us who desire more of the Lord to behold God's glory. Just as the Apostle John invited us to hear, see, handle and otherwise know the manifestation of Jesus Christ (First John 1:1-4), Dale encourages us to engage in this adventure, that our joy may be full.

If you are a lover of the works of John Bunyan and C.S. Lewis, you will want to fill your coffee mug, take a seat in a place where you cannot be interrupted and enjoy the ride found in what is potentially the next classic book from one of the great prophetic writers of our time. I wholeheartedly endorse this book and unreservedly recommend this journey to you!

Dr. Dale Haight

Senior Pastor, Praise Fellowship, Russel, Pennsylvania
Author of *Radical Vessels,* Xulon Publishing

I wept my way through this book! This handbook for pioneer warriors spells out much of my personal journey. If you happen to be on the same journey, then you will surely want to read *Spirit Wind.* Let it be a guide for you along the way. Thank God, the Lord doesn't leave us in the dark. We are the "children of the day." At times we are not sure just what is happening to us and where the Lord is taking us in our experiences. Then He raises up some prophetic scribe, gives him an accurate vision explaining our God activities, and has him record it for our admonition. Dr Dale Fife, my friend, is one of those scribes. God has wonderfully used him here. Read this book prayerfully. Then read it again and again. You will be greatly blessed, as I have been.

James Erb

Senior Pastor, Pleasant Valley Evangelical Church, Niles, Ohio
Founder and President of Antioch International Ministries
Author, *Formed in the Furnace,* Image of God Publications

This is an incredible book written by a friend of God. It swept me off my feet. I couldn't stop reading, and I didn't want it to end. Like a modern Enoch,

Endorsements

Dr. Fife takes us on a journey through eternal realities. Once you are introduced to Spirit Wind, your own spirit will soar as you travel through Frontier Town. Adventure and mystery, surprise and revelation will great you at every turn. You will soon find yourself saying over and over, as I did, "This is about me. This is me! I've been here myself."

After reading *Spirit Wind, The Hidden Kingdom,* and rereading *The Secret Place* more times than I can remember, I can't wait for the next release from Dr. Fife's Secret Place Journal. Don't put this book down until you are all the way through it, and then pray with me for the release of more revelation from this modern prophetic scribe.

Michael A. Bartalone

Founding pastor of Lakewood Chapel and Eagle Rock Church
Cleveland, Ohio
Apostolic overseer
Radio teacher on *The Word for You, The Voice of the City* and *The Gatekeepers*

If you have ever been weary of religious rites or if you have ever asked yourself, "Who am I and why am I here?" then you've come to the right place to learn more. Discover where you might be in the Lord's scheme of things. It's a place where nothing is as it seems. The insights and lessons that Dr. Fife has logged into his field manual within these pages are truly priceless gold nuggets relevant for us all today. Allow *Spirit Wind* to take you to familiar, yet surprisingly different places in the spirit realm where we are reminded that God's ways are not our ways. You will journey to new places just waiting to be explored as the vision of Frontier Town unfolds. Your understanding of heaven's angelic activity and the ways of God will be enlarged as doors of revelation are opened for you and your eyes are opened to see the astounding diversity of God's nature – simple, humorous and altogether mysterious.

Gary and Lynn Brooks

In His Image Ministries
Candler, North Carolina

I'm convinced that every believer has an open heaven available, a place where we can meet with the God of the universe, gleaning incredible insights into the spiritual realm which then enable us to move toward our destiny with a deeper clarity of God's call on our lives. Dr. Fife has the ability to transport the reader into another time and place while teaching us the lessons for the reason of our spiritual existence. And all the while, we are having fun! He has found a portal to "The Well of His Presence" and not only helps us to understand what he's learned there, but encourages us to discover it for ourselves. As he lavishly paints the picture of what he sees on Main Street, you'll find that you suddenly stop reading the words on the pages and instead begin to watch the story unfold in your mind's eye. You simply must take this exciting journey to Frontier Town, but stay alert: "Things are never what they appear to be."

Tricia Menges

Playwright and Producer
Contributing writer of the award-winning situation comedy *Pastor Greg*

Dr. Fife declares, "Frontier Town is more than a vision to me; it is a spiritual reality!" As I read *Spirit Wind: The Ultimate Adventure* I began to understand exactly what he meant. At first I merely longed to be there too, riding on the back of Spirit Wind and experiencing the same powerful and intense instructional encounters that he did. And then ... *I was there!*

Dale is a master wordsmith and a modern seer who is able to cause deep spiritual truths to spring to life through his writing. Chapter Eleven vividly describes the pain we experience at the hands of the Potter. I was powerfully ministered to as a pastor. It brought healing in areas of my own life that I wasn't even aware needed to be dealt with. My prayer is that Dr. Dale Fife, "friend of God...one who walks with the Son," will continue to allow the Holy Spirit to teach us through his gift.

Rev. Carol Missik

Senior Pastor, Living Word Church, Hermitage, Pennsylvania

"Get ready for the next adventure! Dr. Dale Fife has done it again. His gift of storytelling and imagery is amazing! First it was *The Secret Place*, then *The*

Endorsements

Hidden Kingdom and now *Spirit Wind*! The journey on Spirit Wind is incredible and breathtaking! From the moment you arrive in Frontier Town you know that you are in another world. Things are not what they seem to be. The meanings behind the images are far more profound than meets the eye. The spiritual truths and nuggets found in these pages will change the way you view life as a believer. You will find that Frontier Town is a place of new friends, surprises, wonder and majesty. It is also a place of preparation and equipping; best of all, it is a place where you will encounter the Lord, The Well of His Presence and discover who you really were meant to be in Him, an end-time warrior! By the time you finish reading it you will realize that "the end is just the beginning!" I'll see you in Frontier Town.

Apostle John W. Stevenson
Senior Pastor, Heirs Covenant Church of Cincinnati

Many end-time warriors in training have been in a place of hearing, shaking and continued standing despite the temptation to give up on intimacy with our Lord. Their personal destinies are still waiting to be fulfilled. If you are one of these warriors, then *Spirit Wind* is a book that will restore your strength, humility, confidence, resolve, joy and so much more.

This book is marinated in the reality of the love of Christ for you. Reading it will result in an infusion of strength deep into your heart and soul. Fresh revelations and confirmations will become a reality, and your spirit's priority will be renewed in the process.

Dr. Fife is someone who has personally gone through the olive-crushing process. As I read this manuscript it was obvious to me that this book has taken the glory of our Lord within Dale's life to a new level. The Son has powerfully and lovingly worked within his journey of formation. I am humbled, strengthened and exuberant for the work that has been found within him. *Spirit Wind* is the result.

This book is like oil poured forth. It will anoint your soul and penetrate your being, producing restored love! I believe that God will use *Spirit Wind* as one of His instruments to do the same for all of His children.

Briskilla Zananiri

Abana Ministries

Charlotte, North Carolina

When my good friend Dale Fife asked me to read his latest manuscript, *Spirit Wind,* I was filled with anticipation. First, because his books, *The Secret Place, Passionately Pursuing God's Presence* and *The Hidden Kingdom, Journey Into the Heart of God,* were such a blessing; and secondly because this book unfolds in a spiritual place called Frontier Town, a place where I have lived in my heart for years. Accompanying Dale on his journey as a spiritual pioneer in Frontier Town and discovering its unfolding mysteries was life-changing for me. Dale's prophetic insight and gift of storytelling makes this book an important adventure for each of us. The thrill and delight of discovering the many truths that bring us to maturity in God's Kingdom in Frontier Town are priceless. Every Christian should read and treasure *Spirit Wind: The Ultimate Adventure.*

Don Richter

Founder and Director, Harvest Preparation International Ministries

Sarasota, Florida

This book is dedicated to
Bishop Joseph Garlington,
my mentor, friend, traveling companion
and
one of the best storytellers in the world.

TABLE OF CONTENTS

FOREWORD

All too often in our Christian experience we reduce the rich texture of life in the Spirit to a set of rules and regulations. The end result is routine without renewal. God's deepest desire is to have direct experience with each of us, and He has built us for just that. He jealously guards that kind of relationship with every one of His children. When He made us in His image, He gave us the power to imagine. Imagination isn't simply making something up that isn't real, however. True imagination, in the tradition of C.S. Lewis, for instance, is the power to intuitively see into the larger and greater world of the invisible, with all that it contains, and translate it through a series of images, perceptions and cognitions into the language that our human experience can understand.

Before we were converted we were human beings endeavoring to have a spiritual experience. Once we are regenerated we actually become spiritual beings having a human experience. Our life is in the spirit. As such, we are in daily contact with the greater unseen, yet real, world. In that world there are angelic powers and thrones, dominions and authorities, as well as demonic principalities, powers, world rulers of darkness and spiritual forces of wickedness. The unsuspecting soul can be totally unconscious of how much is affecting her or his life on a daily basis unless he maintains ongoing communication and intimacy with the Father of lights, in Whom there is no shadow of turning.

My friend and brother, Dale Fife, is a brilliant communicator of spiritual truth and spiritual reality. His journey with the Lord has deepened his rich understanding of life in the Spirit, and he continually endeavors to invite others on that journey with him. His seamless writing style combined with his intuitive ability to see into the world of the spirit, hear from the world of the spirit and speak the language of that world in a way that we can comprehend causes us to enter into a deeper and more relevant experience with the One who called us to share His intimacy with even those whom we might at first be reluctant to even consider worthy of such.

This brand new release will set you on the road of a pioneer in the spirit and the walk of faith into a world where eternal values are essential to spiritual well being. You'll encounter angels, and father Abraham, and people and places in Frontier Town that are a whole lot like you and me. As a matter of fact, you might even find yourself there in one of the many places that Dale was invited to visit. You'll discover how often your judgments cause you to partake of the law of sin and death and block you from the law of the Spirit of Life in Christ Jesus. You'll discover once again, as if for the first time, how deep and abiding the love of Christ is for His sheep both found and lost.

You'll be reading something of an allegory; yet in true form and fashion you will be encountering the invisible world from which you derive your being. My prayer as you read this book is that it will break you out of any sense of routine and bring you into streams of refreshing and renewal in terms of direct experience with God. Every once in a while as you are reading, pinch yourself just to make sure you are still in the room and haven't wandered into worlds unknown, just to prove to yourself that you are part of a world that is not only in front of your eyes, but a world behind your eyes that is so vast it will take eternity to explore.

Dr. Mark J. Chironna
Author, teacher, musician, television host
Overseer, The Master's Touch International Church, Orlando, Florida

INTRODUCTION

The *Poustinia,* or House of Prayer, overlooks a sequestered lake near the coastal town of Stonington, Connecticut. A single lane gravel road provides the only access into the lodge. There is no television, telephone or potable water. The only neighbors are birds and animals. You don't come here for a vacation; you come to be alone and to pray. That's why my wife and I were so excited about the opportunity. It had been a busy summer of travel and ministry that afforded us little occasion to get alone with God. We were both eager to spend a few days in His presence.

It was an early autumn afternoon when we arrived. The sun filtered through the dappled New England trees, painting the steep hillside and the path leading to the small cabin in harvest hues of faded green, yellow, brown and golden red. Within minutes we were settled into our Spartan accommodations.

Eunice headed for the side porch, her Bible and notebook in hand, to catch the last bit of sun. I claimed the deck overlooking the lake and adjusted the table and chairs for my comfort and convenience. I set my journal and pen on the table and took a seat. The view was breathtaking.

SPLASHDOWN

I bowed my head. "Lord, it's so good to be here alone in Your ..." Before I could finish the sentence, a muted, honking sound skipped across the water shattering the silence. I scanned the distant shore of the lake trying to locate the disturbance. It grew steadily louder until finally a flock of Canada geese came into view, soaring over the lake in 'V' formation like a squadron of bombers looking for a place to land. I watched in delight as they made several investigatory circles over the lake in front of the cabin as though they were waiting for permission from the control tower.

The formation banked toward me, flew overhead, then circled back toward the opposite shoreline. They came in low, legs outstretched like landing gear, feathers set at full flaps, honking like the stall warning horn on a Cessna. Splashdown was awkward, noisy and beautiful. It made me think of what my flight instructor once told me after an unusually bad landing: "Any landing you walk away from is a good one."

The geese trumpeted back and forth at each other as though they were taking roll call, and then a calming silence returned to the woods.

"Lord," I prayed, "that's just how I feel. I've been so busy. Our arrival here was just like these geese. Splashdown was awkward, but I can already feel Your peace settling into my spirit. I dedicate these next few days to You, Jesus. I am here to walk with You like Enoch did. Open my spiritual eyes and ears. Speak to me, Lord. I'm listening."

Instantly, the spontaneous vision of a town appeared. I grabbed my journal and began to copy the images as fast as I could. Within minutes, I had filled several pages with sketches and notes.

"What is this place, Lord?" I asked, staring intently at the drawings in my journal with the eagerness of an explorer charting his course on a map.

"This is Frontier Town," He replied. "In the coming days, I am going to bring you here in the spirit. There are many things that I want to teach you. You will discover them all in this supernatural place."

Those few moments in His presence were the beginning of one of the most incredible spiritual adventures of my life. In the short period of three weeks I recorded several hundred pages of revelation in my journal as the Holy Spirit unfolded the mystery of Frontier Town and unlocked its secrets. This book is the account of the vision as I experienced and recorded it in The Secret Place.

SEEING IS BELIEVING

Literary critics would never classify C. S. Lewis as a prophet, but in my opinion, he was! He had the wonderful gift of vision, the ability to see with the imagination. Like all good writers, he was able to see the story before he wrote it. "All my seven Narnia books, and my three science fiction books began with seeing pictures in my head," said Lewis.[1]

Our sanctified imagination is the page that God uses to write His revelation upon; it is the screen that captures images from the fourth dimension, the realm of His Spirit. Memory deals with our past, conscience helps us cope with the present, but imagination opens amazing horizons and incredible worlds that can only be seen and explored with inward eyes. To see the unseen, to discover the secret, mysterious, wonderful dimension of God's Spirit; that is the privilege and destiny of God's children.

HEAVENLY CREATURES

Angels exist in this unseen world. Every now and then, one of us gets a glimpse of a feather, feels the brush of an unseen hand, or is honored by the appearance of one of God's messengers. We are not alone! Angels are real. The Bible mentions angels over three hundred times. If you believe the Bible, you believe in angels.

Dr. Billy Graham writes, "Angels speak. They appear and reappear. They feel with apt sense of emotion. While angels may become visible by choice, our eyes are not constructed to see them ordinarily any more than we can see the dimension of a nuclear field, the structure of atoms, or the electricity that flows through copper wiring."[2]

In my first two books, *The Secret Place* and *The Hidden Kingdom*, I describe the appearance of angels. I didn't see them with my physical eyes, but in the spirit I knew they were present. It wasn't until the Lord released the vision of Frontier Town that these wonderful beings became individuals to me with names and personalities. They are warriors and guardians, messengers and encouragers. Their powers are beyond human imagination. Their presence is reassuring and comforting. You will meet them in the pages of this book.

SPIRIT WIND

ONE MAN'S JOURNEY

This volume is the account of one man's subjective journey to a prophetic place called Frontier Town. It is the result of my passionate pursuit of God's presence. I gladly acknowledge my weaknesses. I claim no special inspiration. I am not saying, "This is the way it is!" Rather, I'm saying, "This is the way I saw it in the spirit!" My sole desire is to be faithful to the Lord Jesus Christ and His Word. Without apology, I hold fast to the inerrancy and infallible inspiration of the Holy Scriptures. The Bible is the only absolute standard by which this, and all prophetic revelation, must be tested and judged.

SADDLE UP!

Jesus came to set us free from our three-dimensional limitations. He invites us to become pneumanauts, sailors of the Spirit, discovering the underlying reality called truth.[3] C. S. Lewis put it this way, "At Ransom's waking something happened to him which perhaps never happens to a man until he is out of his own world: he saw reality, and thought it was a dream."[4]

Saddle up, partner! We're off to Frontier Town, a place in the spiritual realm where God prepares all of His servants for the end times! Keep your spiritual eyes open wide. I'm certain you will recognize the landscape. Whether you know it or not, if you're passionate for God's presence and radically committed to His purpose, you've been there already; you just didn't realize it. This truly is the final frontier! You're in for the ride of a lifetime. The dream is about to begin. … Or is it reality?

"The wind blows where it wishes, and you hear the sound of it,
but cannot tell where it comes from and where it goes.
So is everyone who is born of the Spirit."
John 3:8

Chapter One

THE PROPHETIC SCRIBE

"I know I'm here by divine appointment," I said, ignoring the intense heat radiating from the bright television lights directly above me and the beads of sweat forming on my brow. Christians from many states and nations were jammed into the church in Charlotte. I sat in the crowded auditorium sandwiched tightly between two people I didn't know. The prophetic conference was in full swing.

I sat riveted to the speaker's words as practical insight and wisdom poured forth from one of God's authentic prophetic voices in the church today. I focused my attention on every statement, not wanting to miss a single kernel of truth.

"How blessed I am to be here," I prayed silently. "What a privilege it is to receive teaching and insight from mature, seasoned leadership regarding the prophetic calling and ministry. I really want to be a more effective servant in Your Kingdom, Jesus."

WRITE THE VISION!

Quite unexpectedly, what for some listeners was simply a casual reference to a specific Scripture as a proof text became a life-altering revelation to me. The speaker's words penetrated deep into my spirit as though they were being written with a supernatural laser pen in the hand of God. *"Therefore, indeed, I send you prophets, wise men, and scribes..."* (Matthew 23:34)

SPIRIT WIND

It was a Matrix moment! Everything around me went into slow motion. My pulse pounded like a sledge hammer, driving home the message with exclamation point power. The Lord was speaking directly to me.

"Yes, Lord! That's it!" I exclaimed, with exploding comprehension. "Now I understand more clearly what Habakkuk meant when he described his experiences in Your presence."

The Old Testament prophet's journal scrolled through my mind like words on a teleprompter. *"I will stand my watch and set myself on the rampart, and watch to see what He will say to me... Then the Lord answered me and said: 'Write the vision and make it plain on tablets, that he may run who reads it. For the vision is yet for an appointed time; but at the end it will speak, and it will not lie. Though it tarries, wait for it; because it will surely come, it will not tarry'"* (Habakkuk 2:1-3) .

"That's exactly what happens to me when I sit in my prayer chair in Your presence for hours at a time, Lord," I said with fresh insight. "Just like Habakkuk, I'm watching to see what You will say to me so I can write the vision for others to read. My journal is like a scroll written in Your presence in The Secret Place."

THE SEERS

A lecture from years past flashed into my memory. The scene was as vivid as though it had just occurred moments ago. My staunch, German Old Testament Prophets professor demanded strict attention from all of his students. His militarily perfect crew cut and the black patch on his right eye gave him a menacing appearance. You simply did not daydream in his class! You were too scared.

Laying his swagger stick on the podium, he opened his lecture notes and peered out of his good eye with the command of a German officer who had just stepped off of the battlefield. When he spoke, we listened.

"There are three different words used for *prophet*," he began. "We find all three of them in First Chronicles 29:29. *'Now the acts of King David, first and* *last, indeed they are written in the book of Samuel the **seer** [ro'eh], in the book of Nathan the **prophet** [nabi], and in the book of Gad the **seer** [hozeh].'*

"The two words translated *seer* emphasize the means by which the person communicated with God, but do not identify these men as being anything different from prophets."[1]

In all three instances, Samuel, Nathan and Gad wrote what they saw and heard God saying. Their quills became instruments of revelation and illumination. Their books reveal God's will and strategy for past and future events. They were prophetic scribes.

GOD STILL SPEAKS

God has not changed! He is the same yesterday, today and forever. On the day of Pentecost, He sent the Holy Spirit to illuminate and enlighten us with prophetic vision.[2] He still anoints and uses prophetic scribes today, inviting them to wait in His presence, write what they see and deliver it to the body of Christ.

As I minister throughout the world, I encounter individuals everywhere who tell me that God has called them into His presence. **Behind the closed doors of their own secret places, these men, women and children are filling their journals with revelation, vision and prophetic insight.**

God has not changed! He is the same yesterday, today and forever.

I regularly receive emails, letters and excerpts from these budding modern-day scribes who seek my input regarding the dreams and visions they have written. The most frequent comment I hear is, "When I read your books, *The Secret Place* and *The Hidden Kingdom*, I realized that I'm not crazy after all. Finally, someone has authenticated my experience. God really is speaking to me."

Have no doubt! God is still speaking to you! Jesus said, *"I still have many things to say to you, but you cannot bear them now. However, when He, the Spirit of truth, has come, He will guide you into all truth; for He will not speak on His own authority, but whatever He hears He will speak; and He will tell you things*

*to come. He will glorify Me, for He will take of what is Mine and declare it to you.
All things that the Father has are Mine. Therefore I said that He will take of Mine
and declare it to you"* (John 16:12-15).

Indeed, God is giving to this generation prophets, wise men and scribes.
We do well to read the vision they have recorded in His presence so that we
may run with renewed zeal in these final days of spiritual harvest.

THE WELL OF HIS PRESENCE

A few days after the prophetic conference as I sat in quiet meditation
before the Lord, the Holy Spirit drew my attention to something I had written in my journal several weeks before I arrived in Charlotte. This revelation
took on much greater significance in the light of my new understanding and
calling to watch to see what He would say to me, write the vision and make it
plain, just as the prophetic scribes did centuries ago.

The vision took place at The Well of His Presence.[3] The discovery of this
well is indelibly etched upon my spirit. It has become more than merely an
image or a vision to me. It is a special place in the spiritual realm where all of
the Lord's people are invited to come to commune with Him and to draw from
the deeper waters of revelation in His Spirit. It is far more than the well of *salvation*; it is The Well of His *Presence*! (See Isaiah 12:3, 55:1.) How wonderful
to know that we are invited to drink from its depths. This is the place where I
come to spend time with Him. Revelation, mystery and truth are all waiting
to be discovered in the well. He is always waiting there to commune with us.

VESSELS OF REVELATION

I stood near The Well of His Presence watching in amazement. An astounding array of vessels, some filled with water from the well and others new and
unused, were scattered on the ground around the circular fieldstone structure.
Gillar and Mannor,[4] the two angels who faithfully accompany me on my Enoch
walks with the Lord, were tending them.[5] They chattered back and forth with
animated excitement, obviously happy that I had returned to the well.

Not paying me any further attention, they continued their work diligent-ly placing objects in each of the vessels. Most of these objects were gleaming precious and semi-precious stones. When the angels dropped them into the vessels, the jewels seemed to come alive, glistening inside their prophetic containers. On rare occasions some intriguing tools, whose uses were unknown to me, were gently laid inside the pitchers. I was mortified when one of the angels placed a small, dry, chalk-white bone into one of the water pots, but then I remembered that God used the power of Ezekiel's prophetic proclamation to make dead, dry bones live again. (See Ezekiel 37:1-10.)

The angels appeared to be cataloguing every water jug by what they placed inside it, stopping often to make careful notations in a booklet lying on top of the stone well. Even the empty vessels were classified so that when that particular revelation was released from The Well of His Presence the appropriate container would be ready. *Every prophetic revelation is given for a specific purpose,* I thought, watching in fascination.

GOD'S PROPHETIC PENS

A large, gold-covered box sat on a table about ten yards to the right of the well's opening just beyond the perimeter of the collected vessels. Pausing from his work, Mannor stood upright and stepped purposefully to the chest. He opened the ancient container with great respect. The top of the box folded open like the keyboard cover on an upright piano. White radiance came cascading out of its interior like light escaping through an open window into a darkened room, engulfing everything within its reach.

I stared in astonishment. "It's a writing table! And the chest is completely full of golden writing instruments!" I gasped, with the delight of a scribe.

"Mannor," I whispered, "they're just like the golden pen you gave me before, the one I used to write *The Secret Place* and *The Hidden Kingdom*.[6] The first time I held the instrument in my hand it created an unforgettable sensation of inspiration."

A tingling anticipation surged through my body. *Could the Lord be preparing me to receive a new writing instrument?* I wondered with hopeful expectancy.

SPIRIT WIND

Perhaps there is a new prophetic revelation waiting to be released from The Well of His Presence.

Mannor examined the golden writing instruments with the trained eye of an expert craftsman checking to see which one was ready. Each pen was made of polished gold and measured approximately a foot in length. The hollow metal cylinders were open at both ends. Each tube was actually a scroll; when you write with the sacred pens your words are inscribed on the interior surface of the cylinders.

He is also a messenger, I thought, watching the angel with admiration. *He understands the need to have the finest, most appropriate writing instrument. Only the pen chosen and appointed by God will be up to the task of recording the vision.*

He paused, pondering his duty. With a pensive look in his eye, he turned his head to the left and gazed off into the spiritual distance, no doubt considering which one he should withdraw and present to me. On command, he returned his attention to the chest and gently touched one cylinder near the top of the carefully stacked scrolls with great respect and reverent care; then he slowly closed the lid.

AN EXPENSIVE STYLUS

"It won't be long," Mannor said, looking at me. "The time is very close. It is almost ready to be…" He paused, considering carefully his choice of words. "Imparted."

I had expected him to say, "Released!"

Detecting my surprise, he quickly responded, "You know better. You will *become* the revelation."

Tears of understanding welled in my eyes. "Yes," I nodded. "I remember well. There's a price to pay for all who receive the anointed pens, but it is a small price compared to the joy of His presence."

Mannor was eager to get back to work cataloguing the vessels around the well. He bent over a large vessel in the middle of the collection and turned his head to look up at me. He gave an encouraging smile, alleviating my apprehension.

"You do understand," he said. **"The prophetic revelation that issues from The Well of God's Presence is expensive, but it is life-giving and life-transforming."**

Chapter Two

DEEPER IN THE WELL

The activity around the well intensified as the angels quickened their pace. *They've been working all this time knowing that I would return, but they must need to finish soon so they will be ready for a new assignment,* I suspected, watching their concentrated efforts.

Gillar looked over at me and then playfully whispered something to Mannor. They both began to laugh. I thought I overheard Gillar say, "I don't think he knows."

"What's wrong?" I asked.

Gillar pointed at my clothes.

I quickly realized why they were laughing. My appearance was appalling. "Oh, Lord," I said, embarrassed. "I didn't realize how unsuited I am to be in Your holy presence. My clothes are wrinkled and dirty. I haven't shaved for days," I said, rubbing my hand across my grubby chin. "I'm a mess! The enemy has really done a job on me. I've neglected my time with You and it shows. Forgive me, Lord."

Thank heaven my appearance did not seem to deter Gillar and Mannor. They went cheerfully about their further preparations. "At least I provided them with a good laugh," I chuckled, somewhat relieved.

NEW VESSELS

Several new angels unexpectedly arrived at the well with a generous shipment of empty vessels. Gillar and Mannor greeted them with surprised inquisitiveness.

"We have been assigned as messengers and servants to assist the multitudes of God's children who will soon be arriving here at the well. There are many more of us on the way," they explained, hastily placing the pots on the ground.

"A few of these vessels are for the one who stands nearby," one of the angels said, pointing toward me, "but the majority of them are for others that the Lord is expecting soon."

The four angels busily attended to the empty vessels, placing them in proper sequence and checking to ascertain that each one contained a single, cataloguing item. I noticed them reading symbols embossed in the clay surface of each vessel.

"This must be how the angels know where to position them," I said softly, not wanting to interfere with their concentration. "There is an obvious plan and strategy in Your mind and heart, Lord. Your orderliness and timing is impressive."

PROPHETIC PERSPECTIVE

I stared in admiration at the growing collection of vessels, some filled with water from The Well of His Presence, glowing with the truth and wisdom of the Almighty, and others still waiting to be lowered into the depths of His knowledge for further revelation.

This is amazing. The prophetic purpose of God from the foundations of creation to the present moment and beyond is gathered right here before my very eyes, I thought. God's calendar is marked, not by days and months, but by the timely release of prophecy to His people. The history of the Father's purpose is made known by the chronology of His revealed mysteries. Surely the Lord God does nothing, unless He reveals His secret to His servants the prophets. (See Amos 3:7.)

This is God's cosmic calendar, I realized. It is a holy chronology that declares God's eternal purpose from out of the pre-creation darkness to the blazing culmination of all things. This is the voice of God spoken in the secret place to His servants, the prophets. This is the revealed mystery of life and divine intention. Only spiritual eyes can discern these truths.

A SUPERNATURAL LIBRARY

Gillar turned in my direction. "It's all here," he said with sage-like affirmation. "This is the collection of God's secrets and mysteries, the strategies and chronicles of war and peace, passionate love and divine wisdom, intrigue, tragedy and comedy, counsel and medical solutions. What you see here is a *library* of God's wisdom drawn from the heart of the Father."

"Indeed, Gillar," I said in agreement. "These are not the mere words of man's wisdom like those once assembled in the great library of ancient Alexandria in Egypt. This is a repository of God's prophetic scrolls, the revelation given to prophets and seers and recorded by prophetic scribes. These scrolls are meant to be read by small and great, rich and poor, powerful and weak alike."

What stood before me at The Well of His Presence far exceeded the genius of men. Even Solomon in all of his attempts to gain knowledge and wisdom palled in the light of this vast array of truth and revelation from the Creator.

God loves His creation, especially mankind. He wants to speak to us. His voice has always been available and remains constant even today. He is not a respecter of persons. He rewards those who seek His face with secrets that are only shared with close friends.[1] What is so amazing is that He chooses to speak to His people through human channels.

THE WIND OF THE SPIRIT

A gentle breeze blew across the vessels of revelation. The voice of the Lord spoke from out of the wind. "I long to communicate with My children. I long to communicate with My children." The words kept repeating with reassuring power. It was a holy invitation to every person to take the time to listen for His voice.

I wondered if the voice of the Spirit could be heard by those passing by the hidden entrance to the well on the road of life nearby.[2] I knew that it would be faint at best and only those who paid careful attention would hear it.

Mannor looked at me in approval. I quickly realized why. My appearance had changed. I was clean shaven and my clothes were fresh. I wiggled my toes inside my tightly laced shoes. The leather shepherd's bag that the Lord had given me for my journey into the Hidden Kingdom was now fastened to my belt with the cup and eye salve safely inside. My sword hung snugly in its sheath on my right side.[3]

DON'T FORGET THE SONG

"My son, don't forget My love song," Jesus said. "The most important gift I have given you is the song that I sang to you months ago when we walked together toward the Hidden Kingdom." [4]

Pure, uninhibited emotion overwhelmed my soul and spirit as the recollection of Jesus singing to me flooded over my being. "How wonderful," I said. "I will always remember how much You love me, Jesus! 'I am my Beloved's, and He is mine," I sighed. "I am loved!"

The assurance of God's love settled into my spirit. I could feel my body relaxing with the awareness of absolute acceptance. His song was only momentary, but its effect was lasting reassurance. Peace pervaded my soul. God had answered my prayer, cleansing and renewing my mind, and replacing my soiled, spiritual garments with clothing suitable for the journey ahead.

A NEW COMMISSION

"He is ready now," Gillar said, as the song of the Lord faded. Gillar and Mannor approached the chest containing the golden writing instruments. Mannor raised the lid and held it open. Gillar carefully lifted the golden scroll from its resting place. The moment he withdrew it from the box its appearance changed. A crimson drop of blood dripped onto the surface of the scroll. It glistened in the sunlight like molten wax. The royal blood confirmed that the scroll was commissioned and approved by God. It is the official seal of the King of kings.

"We will go with you," Gillar and Mannor said in unison, as they approached me with the prophetic writing instrument. "Our work is finished here for now. We have been assigned to accompany you on this new journey of revelation. We have not been this deep in the well before, but the Lord has promoted us in rank and prepared us," Gillar said.

I wasn't sure what he meant by "prepared," but I figured that the Lord had given them special knowledge which qualified them for the task ahead.

"We are guardians of the revelation and your servants. You are greatly loved by the Lord," Mannor said. He placed his hand on my shoulder as a sign of his faithfulness to keep watch and stand guard. Strength and purity reflected in his eyes.

DEEPER INTO THE WELL OF HIS PRESENCE

Gillar stretched forth his arm and handed me the anointed pen with great regard for its purpose. When he released it, the Holy Spirit spoke. "Take great care what you write with this sacred instrument, son. The things that you will see and hear by the Spirit cannot be understood through the use of worldly wisdom.[5] They will make no sense to those without spiritual eyes and ears to see and hear. Do not allow human reason or thought to influence you. Things are not what they first appear to be in My Kingdom!" He emphasized.

"Be careful to write exactly what you see and hear. I will guide you. Obey my leading and follow the gentle impressions that I make upon your spirit."

The things that you will see and hear by the Spirit cannot be understood through the use of worldly wisdom.

THE JOURNEY AWAITS

I wonder what new and amazing mysteries are ahead in The Well of His Presence? I pondered, with anticipation igniting my deepest emotions. The explorer in me came alive; but to my dismay, the vision faded and the presence of the Lord gradually lifted. I instinctively knew that my Enoch walk was over for that day. It was time for me to leave The Secret Place. I would have to wait until tomorrow to return to The Well of His Presence.

Chapter Three

FRONTIER TOWN

I have always loved the secluded atmosphere of my very own Secret Place, but today it sparkled with such iridescent clarity that my spiritual acuity was sharpened beyond my normal perception.

"You are the light-giver, Lord," I prayed. "I am here to walk with you like Enoch did thousands of years ago. Speak to me, Holy Spirit; show me what you want to say. Enlighten my spiritual eyes with Your truth."

In an instant, I was immersed in The Well of His Presence.[1] The vision of Frontier Town that the Lord had revealed to me at the *Poustinia* just a few days before appeared instantly.

WELCOME TO THE WEST

I found myself standing on an arid, open plain in the American West. In the distance I could see the rugged main street of Frontier Town. A raised wood-plank sidewalk stretched the entire length of the street in front of the typical stores, businesses and houses that you would expect to find in such a place. What really confused me, though, was that the town was brand new and freshly painted. It and I seemed out of place chronologically. The scene strangely resembled a theatrical set specifically designed and constructed for a Western movie.

SPIRIT WIND

"I know I am in the twenty-first century, Lord," I said, puzzled by the dilemma. "What possible significance could this newly built frontier town in the Old West have for this post-modern generation?"

THE PIONEERING SPIRIT

"The day and hour has arrived," He replied, with earthshaking authority. "I am about to restore a pioneering spirit in My people. It is like the determination that rested upon Joshua and Caleb and made them want to take the high ground even in their old age. My end-time anointing will enable this last generation to complete My Kingdom plan. They will take back from the enemy what those in the past did not conquer and complete what past generations refused to finish.

"These are days of cataclysmic transition," He continued. "My people see the signs of the times and anticipate My return. They live in hope and faith, but they have not fulfilled my assignment. They are like the children of Israel who I delivered out of Egypt; they embrace My salvation, but do not fully possess the spiritual landscape I intend them to occupy.

"My prophets have seen my end-time plan. They have spoken, but their prophetic words of exhortation and warning have not convinced My people to pursue their destiny. My heart aches because My church loves the world more than Me. I will delay no longer! I am commissioning a new generation for possession. The final battle is about to begin.

"I am releasing this anointing upon the youth especially, but there is a remnant from the past generations who know Me and commune with Me in the Secret Place. Many of them will hear the call to become spiritual pioneers. But even among those who hear it, there will be those who prefer the ease of My wilderness provision and will find it difficult to let go of the familiar and possess the fullness of My end-time purpose."

END-TIME WARRIORS

"The call has gone forth. Do you hear it? It is sounding in your spirit. Do you sense the restlessness stirring within you? Your dissatisfaction is My doing.

It is all around you. It pervades My church. It is Spirit-birthed. You are among those who are called to possess the final frontier. You see, it is not a matter of age; it is a matter of yielding your heart to Me. **It is a matter of radical abandon and obedience."**

My spirit reeled with the impact of His words. *A generation of end-time warriors, spiritual pioneers, cataclysmic transition, restlessness and dissatisfaction, radical abandonment; what's it all mean?* Each phrase swirled around in my mind like a tornado of inner conflict tearing at my fleshly desire to preserve a casual Christianity of comfort and convenience.

"We can't go on like this, Lord," I admitted. "This apathy and indifference is destroying us."

"In the days to come," He replied, "I will teach to you about My end time warriors who will conquer new ground and overcome every hardship and all resistance in My name. These are the obedient ones who are radically abandoned to Me. You will find them here in Frontier Town. That is why I brought you to this place."

THE INHABITANTS OF FRONTIER TOWN

I turned my attention back to Frontier Town and the activity on Main Street. I could see people in the distance walking along the wooden sidewalk and unceremoniously entering and exiting the various buildings of the town. It was clear from their friendly greetings that they all knew each other. **Despite the fact that none of them looked familiar to me, I had the strange sense that our paths had crossed before.**

They swaggered with such confidence and strength of purpose that it was obvious to me they were navigating by the bearings of an inner compass of spiritual destiny. They were not self-assured; instead, they demonstrated an incredible, unwavering faith in God. Like any frontier town, these individuals appeared rugged and wary; yet, there was a reassuring peace pervading their countenance. Even though everyone embraced a common purpose, their hardy individualism was refreshing.

"Who are they, Lord? Will I have the opportunity to meet and speak with them?" I asked, determined to unmask the mystery of Frontier Town.

AN ANGELIC COURIER

The shuffling noise of someone scraping his foot in the dirt behind me startled me. I spun around to my right just in time to see an angel approaching. He was carrying an unusual book cradled in his massive hands. He lifted it to chest height and held it out toward the Lord.

"Thank you, Malchior," Jesus said, as He lifted the book from its resting place. The angel gently nodded his head in a reverent gesture that communicated far more than words could. His simple nod revealed his total devotion to Jesus. It was the obedient response of an angel of high rank to his Commander-in-Chief, strong and yet totally yielding.

His actions reminded me of the centurion's words, *"Lord, I am not worthy that You should come under my roof. But only speak a word, and my servant will be healed. For I also am a man under authority, having soldiers under me. And I say to this one, 'Go,' and he goes; and to another, 'Come,' and he comes; and to my servant, 'Do this,' and he does it"* (Matthew 8:8-9).[2]

This same understanding of Kingdom authority exuded from Malchior's behavior. He lowered his arms to his side and stood at ease in the dusty street next to us. His duty fulfilled, he waited for further instructions.

THE MYSTERIOUS BOOK

My focus was riveted on the curious book. I had never seen anything like it. It was square, seven inches in height and width, and almost three inches thick. It had a rugged, sturdy appearance. The binding was a canvas-like, tan cloth, more yellow than brown. The spine seemed especially durable and was clearly made to withstand abuse. Gold gilded the page edges like an expensive Bible. *Why would such a plain, durable volume be embellished with gold-etched pages?* I wondered.

The locking device was stunning. A two-inch wide, leather strap was sewn to the outer edge of the back cover. A pewter buckle, shaped like a lantern with an elongated hole in the center, was fastened to the end of this strap. A diamond studded pin served to secure the buckle tightly against the front cover. The jeweled pin was a miniature, silver sword. When the lantern buckle was placed over the pin and the sword twisted into the locking position the clasp held the book securely closed.

I recognized immediately that this design was symbolic. The locking mechanism was in honor of Gideon. The latch and clasp represented Gideon's lanterns and the sword of the Lord, both implements of faith's warfare.

My eyes frantically searched the small book like a detective looking for clues. *It bears no identifying markings of any kind,* I concluded. *It's rugged and rather plain, obviously designed for use in difficult conditions or terrain. Durable and sturdy, it will hold up in any adverse climate or circumstances; but why the gold pages?*

I couldn't restrain myself any longer. "What kind of book is this, Lord?" I blurted out impatiently.

GOD'S LIBRARY

Jesus turned the silver sword and lifted the lantern buckle from the pin. He opened the book to the first page. *It must be the title page,* I thought, as I pressed closer with unbridled curiosity.

Printed at the very top were strange, mysterious markings in an unfamiliar language. *Is this some sort of code? No, it must be cataloguing of some kind,* I thought, with a burst of insight. *These numbers must classify this particular book as one of a series contained in the multiple volumes of a collection. This book must be from God's library!*

No sooner did the thought occur to me than a scene from a previous journey into The Well of His Presence flashed into my mind. I recalled seeing a door in the Strategy Room of Heaven.[3]

Could that door be the entrance to the sacred library? Is the Holy Spirit revealing some of its contents to me now? I was not allowed to enter it then, but perhaps some day the Lord will grant me permission to explore it, I thought, with the delightful feeling that there could be a Christmas morning in heaven.

ESPRIT-DE-CORPS

A quote written in biblical Greek appeared directly beneath the catalogue markings. *My New Testament Greek class was worth all the effort. It really comes in handy now,* I thought, easily translating the text.[4] *"In the beginning was the Word, and the Word was with God, and the Word was God."* (John 1:1)

Several empty lines separated this Greek inscription from a motto-like phrase boldly printed in English: *"To Conquer, To Love, To Redeem."* Just reading this pledge gave me a marine-like sense of *esprit-de-corps.* Valor, compassion and mission were all power packaged and compressed into these few words. My emotions engaged with tantalizing thoughts of daring adventures and courageous exploits. I felt like a fresh recruit signing up for basic training to become a spiritual warrior.

"I'm willing to face any obstacle for Your Kingdom, Lord!" I said presumptuously, momentarily glancing up from the page into Jesus' face.

THE TITLE

Swallowing hard with resolve, I riveted my attention on the mysterious book. The title drew my eyes like a magnet. The words exploded off the center of the page directly into my spirit with implicit authority: *Field Manual for Spiritual Pioneers.* My head jerked upward instantly. Wide-eyed, my mouth agape, I held my breath, not daring to say a word.

THE AUTHOR'S SIGNATURE

Jesus didn't speak. He cradled the book in his left hand and reached for a pen tucked safely into a plain leather holder inside the front cover. Removing the yellow, three-sided pen, He sat down on the hard, dusty earth and began to write something on the lower right hand corner of the front page. When He finished, He closed the book and handed the pen to Malchior. He stood up, turned to face me, and held out the manual. "Here, son, this copy is for you," He said.

I was ecstatic. My eyes filled with tears of joy. "My very own copy, Lord… This is awesome!" I opened the book with delight and read the inscription. "*To my son, Dale, You are one of my pioneers. To him who overcomes will I give the treasures of heaven. Love always, Jesus.*"

MY PERSONAL COPY

I tightened my grip on the priceless treasure. My heart was so full. My thoughts raced back to when I was a little child. My mother often told others how much I loved books. She would say, "Just give him a book and he'll be happy for hours."

Jesus smiled with the delight of the giver when a gift is well-received.

"I will cherish this book forever," I said. "It is one of my most prized possessions."

Jesus responded, "My son, you are not the only one that I have given a copy of this manual to. This book is not for display in an honored place. It is meant to be used! In the days to come I will guide you through it. Keep it with you. You will find blank spaces in this manual that only you can fill in. At the appropriate time, I will instruct you what to write. Use the golden writing instrument that Gillar gave you to record what I say."

"I understand, Lord," I replied. "I will do as You say and obey the promptings of Your Spirit."

He nodded in approval and then turned away. It was time to leave The Well of His Presence for today. I opened my leather shepherd's bag and placed the field manual inside next to the golden writing instrument. The milkglass container of eye salve clanged against my metal cup as I drew the leather cord snuggly around the pouch. The vision faded.

Chapter Four

MAIN STREET

I threw off the heavy down comforter and headed immediately for my secret place with the abandon of an adventurer eager to explore and experience unknown, uncharted territory. Frontier Town filled my thoughts; yesterday's events strengthened my resolve. My pulse pounded with adrenaline-infused excitement.

The sun was just peeking over the pine covered ridge on the opposite side of the valley when I set my steaming mug of coffee on the table next to my chair. The sight of the inlaid ivory elephants contrasting with the dark rich mahogany of the table reminded me of my recent trip to the major cities of India.

They're real cities, I mused, *but Frontier Town is just as real to me as any place I've ever been in this world. It reminds me of what I heard a friend say, "Engage the imagination; take it where you will.* **People only go to places they have already been in their own minds.** *"*

I will go →

LIFE, **NOT** AS USUAL!

Outside my frosted study window the morning mist hung above the pond next to the church like an ethereal curtain separating me from the highway beyond it and its accompanying crowd of early morning traffic.

The morning rush has already begun, I thought. *People are going about life as usual. But not me, not today; I know that this day will not be usual at all. I've set aside the duties that normally beg for my attention and made room for You in my schedule. This day is entirely devoted to You, Lord!*

I settled into the reflective silence of my prayer chair and opened my journal to the blank page next to yesterday's entry. "I'm back, Lord." I said, inhaling to the limit of my capacity and then slowly, deliberately exhaling while twisting my body to find a more comfortable position. "I'm so excited I can't contain my curiosity. Teach me Your ways, Jesus. Show me Your heart. I'm here to walk with You today like Enoch. I love You so much."

APPROACHING FRONTIER TOWN

In seconds, His presence filled the room and my spiritual eyes were opened. Frontier Town reappeared in the distance. My angelic traveling companions were waiting for me. My hand brushed across the shepherd's pouch at my waist. Beneath the supple leather I could feel the outline of the objects it contained. Everything was exactly where I had left it yesterday. Reassured of the readiness and availability of its sacred contents, I listened closely to Jesus' instructions.

"Today we must view the buildings along Main Street," the Lord said, as He turned toward the single street of Frontier Town. "In the coming days we will enter each building; but today I want us to traverse the entire street together."

We walked side by side at an easy pace. Gillar and Mannor strolled out ahead of us like celestial tourists on vacation. I chuckled as Gillar swaggered to my right in a playful, delightfully unreligious mood. He was thoroughly enjoying the ambiance of the setting, pretending to be an angel cowboy acting on a Hollywood movie set. Mannor was not at all happy about his colleague's irreverent cavorting. Brushing the resulting dust from his robe, he looked at him with a stern, parental expression. His gruff voice shattered the humor of the moment. "This is serious, Gillar. You've gone a little too far. Stop your daydreaming."

Gillar responded as though someone had just poured cold water on him. *I don't think angels pout, but this is probably as close as it gets,* I thought, feeling the disappointment of Gillar's denied playfulness.

Malchior followed our entourage a few respectful paces behind us with a dignity and muscular strength and agility that clearly portrayed his rank and prowess.

As we drew closer to Main Street my attention shifted to the scene unfolding before me. Yesterday, when I first saw Frontier Town, I was standing a considerable distance away, but now as we advanced toward it I could see much more detail. The small settlement was geographically positioned in the center of a wide open, arid, level plain that stretched off in every direction as far as the eye could see. There were no trees anywhere. No mountains could be seen on the horizon, no cactus or Joshua trees dotted the landscape with their sentry-like posture: just level, yellow, dusty dirt encompassed the town, and a few puffy white clouds punctuated the Easter-egg blue sky above it like floating cotton balls.

"Seldom rains here," I said, kicking at the dusty soil under my feet and glancing over at Gillar with an encouraging smile. He grinned back mischievously, immediately understanding my innuendo.

THE STAGE IS SET

The aroma of freshly cut pine filled the atmosphere like a lumberjack's cologne. *Must be a saw mill nearby*, I thought. Then I realized that each house or shop on the single thoroughfare directly ahead was newly constructed and most of them were made of clapboard.

The buildings on Main Street were joined together in a continuous progression by a wide, elevated boardwalk that stretched the length of the town. This walkway provided easy access to each structure. Wooden stairways of varying sizes led from the dirt street onto the decking in front of every doorway.

To my dismay, unlike yesterday, Main Street was now deserted. There were no identifying signs of life. No placards, advertising or billboards hung on the buildings. No rocking chairs or merchandise were positioned on the decking. Horse tracks dotted the street, but not a single tether was provided. But the most surrealistic feature of Frontier Town piqued my curiosity; only one side of Main Street had buildings on it. The whole scene gave the impression that the town was a backdrop for a drama whose scenes were yet to be acted out. I suddenly realized that the plot was just beginning.

But isn't this exactly how God speaks? I reasoned. *Vision is the prophets' language, and story is the teachers' venue. A single street in the middle of a nowhere wilderness called Frontier Town; I can't wait to see what really takes place here on Main Street.*

A CLOSE UP OF MAIN STREET

"You told me that You designed Frontier Town to train and equip your servants, Lord. Where are the people I saw yesterday?" I asked, eager for information.

> *Vision is the prophets' language, and story is the teachers' venue.*

"I will introduce you to them at the appropriate time, son." He replied. "But first you must learn about Main Street. **I have designed every structure here with a specific goal in mind. In the days to come you will learn the purpose and function of each building.** In the process you will meet those who are in town right now."

We walked together in silence up the deserted street. Jesus paused momentarily in front of each of the buildings, but offered no explanation for their purpose. I carefully noted the size and shape of each structure, sometimes venturing a guess at its intended use. Since there were no addresses, I assigned a number to each one for my convenience.

ONE MAIN STREET

The first building was rather small, one story, with a flat roof sloping from front to back. A single door with two paned windows a few feet from either side of the entrance highlighted the otherwise nondescript front wall. A fresh coat of navy-like, grayish-blue paint gave the small wooden structure a crisp, well tended freshness. The white accent trim around the door, windows and corners of the structure added a homey touch.

TWO MAIN STREET

The second structure was quite large; the tallest building on the street. It shared a common wall on the right with the first building, but extended several stories above it. Its bright, soft, yellow paint gave a happy glow to Main Street. Shutter-like swinging doors hung in the otherwise open entrance. On either side of the doorway facing the boardwalk were two very large glass windows. White curtains framed them, hanging in large masculine pleats tied back on the sides with simple matching cord sashes. Someone had traced letters on the upper part of the windows in preparation to paint a sign on them permanently, but I could not determine what they spelled.

A large balcony jutted out over the boardwalk, providing a porch roof above the promenade. This balcony encircled the entire length and breadth of the second story. Several doors led from the walkway into private rooms. The third story was accented by paned windows on both front and side walls. The roof was similar to the first building, sloping from front to back and covered with black tar paper.

THREE MAIN STREET

The third building was a real puzzlement. "I've never seen anything quite like this," I said to myself, wondering what its purpose was. "It's extremely low; hardly more than five feet high," I estimated, "and it's constructed with tongue and grove planking. Looks to me like porch decking placed vertically. Sure would be hard to break into. The absence of windows really looks suspicious. I wonder if some sort of secret activities take place inside."

The short access door was built like the walls and reached to within inches of the flat roof. It was fastened to a sturdy frame with strong, triangular shaped hinges and secured with a cylindrical combination lock that had three dials on it. The dials contained symbols instead of numbers, but the Lord moved on before I could examine them more closely.

Every time I glanced away and then looked back at this structure its width and length appeared to increase slightly. It had a life-like, amorphous quality about it. *Could this be some sort of supernatural shed?* I thought. *You have to stoop just to get in the door and you couldn't possibly stand up straight once inside. And why does its size change?*

FOUR MAIN STREET

Mannor intentionally brushed my arm as we approached the next building. He looked like he was going to explode if he didn't speak; but he restrained himself, not daring to divulge the purpose of the structure.

I wonder what that's all about. There must be something special about this particular building, I thought, stopping to study the mysterious circular edifice entirely covered with wooden shakes. *This is really quite exceptional. It seems peculiarly out of place. It looks like a silo.*

When I first saw this building from a good distance away it appeared to be joined to the rest of Main Street, but now I could see that it stood separate and distinct from the other structures except for a low passageway. A rectangular, windowless tunnel connected the vertical cylinder at its base to the rear of the previous shack about thirty-five feet away. The only way into the silo was through the mysterious shed and the passageway connecting them.

A familiar longing unexpectedly coursed through my spirit. I sensed an overwhelming desire to get to The Secret Place. The Lord smiled and placed His hand on my shoulder. "Do you feel it, son?" He said, confirming what I was sensing and pointing toward the silo.

The unusual building had a powerful allure. In the spirit I discerned that it had windows, but I just couldn't see them. *I wonder if the windows are visible from inside the building, but hidden to those who casually walk by, Like one way glass; if you're inside you can see out, but anyone out here can't see in.*

I had no sooner thought of the hidden windows than the walls of the silo became transparent. I stared in astonishment. A stone well stood in the middle of the circular room. A lantern hung above it on the crossbeam, emitting a holy glow into its depths. A cloud of mist filled the room and angelic beings stood guard around the well.

The revelation exploded within me. "The Well of His Presence," I shouted. "It's The Well of His Presence! **That's why my spirit leapt within me. The**

well has an opening here in Frontier Town. That explains why Mannor brushed my arm; he knew about this.

"Now it makes sense why this building is detached from the wooden sidewalk and separated from the other houses. There's no stairway from the street in front of it on the boardwalk either. Only those individuals who feel its pull and discern its significance will take time to investigate it. But if they do, they will discover its secret and gain access to the well."

I didn't want to go any further. "This building and The Well of His Presence can take me to a million undiscovered places in the spirit," I said, looking over at Mannor. "This is how I got here in the first place."

"But there is still a lot more to see on Main Street," Mannor replied. "We must move on."

FIVE MAIN STREET

The next building had the look and feel of a typical Western general store. Round wooden posts supported a porch roof that extended over the boardwalk. The stark, white building was accented with Kelly green, latticed shutters. Through the front window I could see shelves lining the walls, well stocked with provisions of every kind. A large piece of furniture about the size of a china closet stood in the center of the room. It had small wooden openings on both sides.

"Post office boxes," I said, "apparently for distributing mail to the inhabitants of Frontier Town. But who are they? Sure would like to see the names on those compartments."

SIX MAIN STREET

Gillar and Mannor were eager to proceed. By now I was thoroughly immersed in the fascination of Frontier Town. A delightful white clapboard, one-room schoolhouse was erected adjacent to the store. It sat back from the wooden sidewalk, separated from the buildings on either side by a rich green lawn. The sight evoked visions of children at recess flying kites in a stiff western breeze off the prairie or romping to and fro in playful pursuit with their shirts hanging out and poplin dresses swirling about. But the schoolyard was deserted now – there was not a sound of children playing anywhere.

The stalwart steeple towered overhead, its school bell glistening in the midday sun. Multicolored shafts of light reflected from the surface of the silver object with the brilliance of refracted light cascading from the facets of a diamond. **Squinting up into the light beams, I could tell that the bell was inscribed with etched words, but I couldn't read them from this distance.**

Black shutters hung permanently open at each window and were secured to the exterior walls of the schoolhouse. I peered into the screenless openings. "There's a refreshing clarity inside," I uttered. "The interior of this school really has an atmosphere conducive to learning."

SEVEN MAIN STREET

A typical two-story, frame house, like you might find in any city, sat next to the school house. It had no porch and connected directly to the boardwalk. A center front door and lots of windows provided light for each room. Rather plain and indistinct as it was, I hadn't a clue to its purpose or function. It was partially painted a pilgrim kind of New England gray to a height just above the first story. The abrupt jagged paint line circumnavigating the structure gave the impression that the builder ran out of paint in the middle of the job. Bare wooden walls were exposed the rest of the way to the two-sided roof, which sloped to a peak.

I was puzzled by its unfinished exterior, but I knew how wisely and carefully the Lord builds. Nothing is by accident or without purpose and function. *Time will reveal its enigmatic place in the scheme of things here in Frontier Town,* I thought.

EIGHT MAIN STREET

Turning to explore the next building on Main Street, I suddenly realized that Malchior, Gillar and Mannor were gone. The only trace left of their angelic presence was the outline of footprints in the dusty street. I figured that they must have another important assignment to attend to.

"Just a few more buildings to see," Jesus said, redirecting my attention, but offering no explanation as to the whereabouts of our departed companions.

A cerulean blue, single-story, rectangular building appeared next. Its full length stretched along the boardwalk. I immediately recognized it as a restaurant. White lace curtains hung from rods in the two generous windows on either side of the doorway. Through the spotless window panes I could see a number of round tables inside covered with red and white checkered table clothes. Captain's chairs with red, padded seat cushions encircled the tables. A counter ran the length of the back wall with tall stools randomly spaced along it for groups of customers. A bubbling five-gallon coffee urn sang a barely audible perking song in the far left corner.

I detected the smell of fresh bread baking. Apparently the tempting aroma was coming from the room just beyond the back wall of the establishment. "That smells great," I said, sniffing the delightful scent and salivating with sudden hunger. Wisps of steamy, white smoke puffed intermittently out of the partially open kitchen door just beyond the counter.

NINE MAIN STREET

We were now approaching the far end of Main Street. Only two more buildings remained. Just past the restaurant, an unpainted pinewood structure with a well weathered look sat quite a way back from the boardwalk. Smoke steadily rose skyward from a single stone chimney jutting at least eight feet above the roof's surface.

This must be the blacksmith's shop, I thought, at first sight.

In a few more paces I could see through the large, open, barn-style doors. A white hot oven glowed with superheated brilliance. Huge leather bellows sat next to the fiery furnace.

"This isn't a blacksmith's shop; it's a pottery business!" I declared, as the shelves lining the right wall came into view. All kinds of pottery in various sizes, shapes, colors and phases of completion were stacked in random order along the dusty, bare, wood shelving.

Curious, I thought. *Why would there be a pottery shop here in Frontier Town? I didn't see that many people yesterday. There don't seem to be enough inhabitants to warrant such a business.*

TEN MAIN STREET

We finally arrived at the last building on Main Street at the far end of the boardwalk.

"This place has a distinct pioneering atmosphere to it," I said, glancing over at the Lord. "It's far more rustic than all the others."

"Look carefully," He replied, nodding in agreement.

Built of pine logs, the single story cabin perfectly exemplified the natural frontier look. The naked white tree trunks with their exposed knots glistened under a fresh coat of honey colored lacquer that ran down into the caulking between the logs like rivulets of sticky maple syrup poured over a stack of flapjacks.

To my fascination, the only readable words on the entire street were placarded on the cabin. A small wooden sign hung from a nail next to the door by a leather strap the size of a shoelace. There's no way I could have noticed the sign from a distance. Its color and leather cord blended right into the cabin wall. The sign read "Arriving & Departing." The words appeared directly above their respective columns. The lower part of the sign was designed to accommodate removable letters and numbers that could be changed as necessary.

This must be a calendar of some kind, like a schedule or timetable. I thought. *Maybe this is a stagecoach stop. It's obviously some sort of staging area for the town.*

A CONSTRUCTION SITE

The planked sidewalk ended abruptly at the end of the log cabin. Steps led down to a vacant lot where a pile of lumber lay on the ground in disarray like giant sticks dangling in different directions. Surveyor's stakes had been driven into the dry soil. A single line of string was stretched between the stakes.

Someone must be getting ready to build, I thought with delight. *Construction isn't finished here. New things are happening in Frontier Town. Soon the walls of a new structure will rise right here at the end of Main Street. I wonder what it will be.*

YOUR LIFE WILL BE CHANGED

"Now you have seen Main Street in its entirety," Jesus said. "In the days to come We will visit each of these buildings. In the process your life will be changed! It is critical that you recognize that this is no ordinary town. It is a supernatural place of preparation and equipping for everyone I have chosen and called to be an end-time warrior.

"Each building represents a unique encounter with My Kingdom purposes. Only the committed and courageous can survive here. Many of those whom I invite to this place come willingly, but do not stay. They retreat back into their complacency and chose to settle in a place of spiritual comfort and convenience. They opt for worldly success instead of Kingdom conquest. Do not follow their example. If you persevere I will abundantly reward you just as I reward all of My servants who overcome the tests and challenges of Frontier Town.

"This place is as old as time itself, but always new to those who arrive in each generation. Its function is clear; here is where I train and commission My warriors to possess their spiritual destiny. I will take back all that the enemy has stolen; all of creation is My possession. Ultimate victory is assured. I have come to conquer, to love and to redeem. This is the battle cry of My servants. My Kingdom will come! My will shall be accomplished on earth just as it is in heaven."

THE BATTLE CRY

Jesus' words resounded in my spirit, instantly reminding me of what I had read in the field manual. I quickly reached into my leather bag, grasped the book and thrust it open. The words leapt off the page with new vitality: *"To Conquer, To Love, To Redeem!"*

"This is the battle cry of Your soldiers, Jesus," I stated. "It is the motto of every end-time warrior who is willing to pay the price to possess Your final frontier."

I quickly glanced past the title, *Field Manual for Spiritual Pioneers,* and eagerly turned to the next page. My mouth fell open in astonishment. On the top of the right page were the words, "Table of Contents." Below this title, descending in perfect order, were precise drawings of every building in the same sequence as they appeared on Main Street. The artist's sketches accurately captured the details of each structure in Frontier Town.

THE TABLE OF CONTENTS

The single-story, grayish-blue building with white trim and sloping, flat roof appeared at the top of the column. Below it was a sketch of the yellow, three-story structure with its swinging doors and balcony. Next, the half-story, windowless building that kept changing shape appeared. Its door hinges and lock were accurately detailed in the picture. The silo was directly beneath this shed. Its rainbow colored shingles shimmered like a hologram when I moved my eyes past it to the next drawing of the general store. The white school house; the mysterious, partially painted frame house; and the potter's workshop followed in descending order. Near the end of the column was an exact replica of the log cabin with its unique sign. A blank space appeared at the very bottom of the page to provide room for a final entry. *Could this be the place for the new building under construction?* I wondered.

An empty line appeared adjacent to each picture in the table of contents. I immediately realized that my assignment was to fill in these blanks. I knew intuitively that the Lord would reveal to me in the days to come what descriptive title to give each building. I realized that I would only be able to complete the Table of Contents after I had personally experienced each location.

THE FIRST LESSON

My hand trembled with excitement as I closed the field manual and placed it back in the leather bag. *What discoveries are ahead?* I thought. *What will be required of me in order to learn the purpose and significance of each building? Will I be up to the challenge?* A deep sense of trust in Jesus stirred within me. *Surely He did not bring me here to let me fail,* I reassured myself.

Like a soldier preparing to face the trials of an obstacle course, I reinforced my resolve. "If this place is for training and equipping, Lord, I need Your help. By Your grace and power I can do all things."

"Good!" Jesus said. "You have recognized the key principle. Here in Frontier Town, you must be led by My Spirit. That is the only way you can advance. Your own might and power will not suffice.[2] Tomorrow we will begin your training."

The sun was setting as we made our way back down the street. Gillar stood alone at the far end of Main Street. He was no longer daydreaming. Instead, a look of determination chiseled his face with intention.

"This is going to be some adventure, Lord." I said, as we walked past the last building and on to the open prairie.

"See you tomorrow in Frontier Town, Lord," I called, as darkness descended on Main Street like a curtain on a stage. Today's lesson was over.

Chapter Five

SPIRIT WIND

A new day was just beginning in Frontier Town. I watched in worshipful silence as the beauty of God's creation unfolded above me. The western sky spread over the roofs of Main Street like a watercolor canvas being painted by the masterful hand of the Almighty. The intensifying pastel brilliance poured through the dispersing clouds in a waterfall of orange and violet light heralding the commencement of another day of adventure in this supernatural training ground.

Sunrise in Frontier Town sure does arrive with majestic grandeur, I thought, starring at the thin wispy clouds slowly dissipating into translucent vapor like a curtain rising on a celestial stage. *What does God have in store today?* I wondered. I quickly realized that the answer was on its way!

A WELCOME SURPRISE

Toward the rising sun, well beyond the street and the houses – in the far distance just barely visible on the horizon – a small cloud of dust rose from the plain. It formed a narrow line tinting the distant sky-scape brown.

"A stampede of horses or buffalo might raise such a cloud," I reasoned.

Closer and closer it came like a wind-driven sandstorm, until finally a single horse became visible beneath the cloud. **The regal white stallion galloped toward me with energized grace and authoritative freedom.** His mane rippled in the air like a flag snapping in a stiff breeze. He breathed in a deep, long cadence. Heat from his nostrils produced intermittent puffs of condensation in the morning air. Saddled but riderless, he came steadily on with determined vigor.

I was completely caught off guard. I stared at the approaching horse like someone who had unsuspectingly walked into a room to discover a surprise birthday party. Sudden realization exploded within me. "This is the same white stallion that I saw in The Secret Place months ago on one of my first prophetic journeys," I said, realizing the significance of his arrival.

I recalled every detail of that experience with great delight.[1] The first time I had encountered this majestic steed, we were galloping along an ocean beach in the brilliant sunshine. I will never forget the power and excitement I felt as the water sprayed around us in every direction. There was no saddle or reigns then because Jesus was teaching me an important lesson. I needed to overcome my fear of not being in control. At the very beginning of my prophetic training in The Well of His Presence He was teaching me the vital necessity of trusting the Holy Spirit unquestioningly.

"This white horse represents My Spirit," Jesus told me then. His instruction alleviated my trepidation and gave me great assurance. "You must trust My Spirit to carry you where I want to take you. I desire to move you into deeper places and introduce you to My hidden secrets. Each day will bring a new environment and a new dimension of revelation. Let My Holy Spirit teach you. Allow Him to lead you. He only moves at My command and permission. I will give Him specific instructions concerning you."

THE WIND OF THE SPIRIT

The tempo of hooves gradually slowed to a trot as the stallion approached. Whinnying in the dusty air, he sauntered up to my side and lowered his head, nudging my shoulder with an affectionate shove.

"Welcome," I said, respectfully stroking the side of his neck in one sweeping motion. "You run like the wind!"

Just touching his glistening, white coat sent an overwhelming burst of awe and inspiration through me. "Who is this, Lord?" I asked.

His response came deep inside of me. "This is Spirit Wind! I have sent Him to guide you through Frontier Town."

"Spirit Wind…" I paused. "Then that's what I'll call you," I said, with heartfelt respect. "Lead the way, Spirit Wind!"

GOD'S PERFECT DESIGN

The aroma of leather emanating from Spirit Wind's new saddle filled the surrounding air with the scent of uncommonly expensive luxury. An intricately patterned border was masterfully carved into its outer edges, but what really caught my attention was the saddle horn. Made of rich, smooth, deep-brown leather, its hand-polished finish sparkled like the surface of a mirror. Its seams were stitched with silver thread.

I reached up to grab the horn with my left hand. Placing my left foot into the stirrup, I paused to affirm Spirit Wind's approval and then thrust my full weight onto His muscular frame. "It fits perfectly," I said, inching slightly toward the back of the saddle. With no more than the slightest pressure from my knees, Spirit Wind turned in the predetermined direction and headed toward Frontier Town.

SPIRIT-LED VISION

I had absolute confidence in the ability and wisdom of Spirit Wind. No longer detached beings, we became one entity moving gracefully ahead with unrestrained power and freedom. But if I tried to steer by gently tugging to either side of the horn, he would huff in a tone of resistance and continue on in the direction he was heading. *I shouldn't be surprised,* I thought. *He's obeying another Master.*

I still felt awkward without reigns, but I reminded myself, "I'm better off without them." I leaned forward to grip the saddle horn with my left hand and reached my right arm toward Spirit Wind's muscular neck. I could feel the uncommon strength coursing through his veins. With the slightest pressure of my fingertips, his head bent slightly to the right as if he were saying, "Thank you, My friend." I realized in that instant that communication between us did not require words.

EXPECT THE UNEXPECTED

When we arrived at Main Street I fully expected Spirit Wind to stop in front of the one story, first building at the head of the street. "Whoa…!" I shouted to no avail, as he galloped right past it without even hesitating. Everything within me wanted to stop him, but I remembered the Lord's words, "Trust My Spirit and do not try to control or guide Him."

We charged up the street of Frontier Town leaving a cloud of yellow dust behind us. I could tell that Spirit Wind was enjoying this display of unbridled energy. We passed every building and only slowed to a trot when we came to the last structure on the street. Jesus stood on the road just beyond the board-walk waiting for us. A brand new tethering post that had not existed the day before stood firmly in place at the edge of the street. The single pole had an exquisite carving on top. It was a perfect replica of Spirit Wind.

The royal steed slowed to a walk and stopped in front of the tethering post. Jesus stroked his side and then whispered something in his ear. Spirit Wind stood perfectly still. *He will never move from this spot without a command from the Lord,* I thought.

When I dismounted onto the street of Frontier Town I saw that Jesus was wearing blue jeans.[2] He spoke in an industrious tone like the foreman on a work site. It was immediately clear to me that He had planned our agenda for the day; He was all business. *There's much to learn and experience ahead,* I thought, *I need to pay close attention.*

THE END IS THE BEGINNING

Before I could ask, Jesus began to explain why we were positioned at what I thought was the end of Main Street. "Good morning, son," He said. "We are starting here because this town is like no other you have ever seen. What seems like the beginning is really the end and what appears to be the end is really the beginning. This is true in all of life. My ways are not your ways and My thoughts are not your thoughts.[3] Didn't I say that the last shall be first and the first shall be last?[4] That's how it is here in Frontier Town. What appears obvious to human reasoning is not necessarily so in the spiritual realm."

Jesus' words penetrated my spirit. A scene from the Bible flashed into my thoughts. I could see the prophet Samuel standing in Jesse's house. Each of Jesse's sons was brought before the prophet to be considered as the one chosen by God to become Israel's king. From the eldest to the youngest, Samuel carefully sought God's will, his horn of anointing oil in readiness. None of Jesse's sons passed the test.

What appears obvious to human reasoning is not necessarily so in the spiritual realm.

Finally Samuel, unsettled in his spirit, asked if there were any sons remaining. Jesse replied, "Only David, my youngest; but surely he cannot be the one."

"Call him here!" Samuel retorted.

God chose David, the most unlikely son, to be Israel's next king. Samuel poured the oil of anoint-

ing upon the young shepherd's head. This was the first of three times David would be identified by God's anointing as the chosen one.[5]

"The last shall be first," I affirmed.

Jesus' words brought me back to the moment. "You must be careful how you see things here in Frontier Town. I call women and men to be My spiritual pioneers whom the world and the church think are the least likely or qualified. This is contradictory to the logic of men, but those who have prophetic discernment, like Samuel the prophet, understand that I do things differently."

NEVER ASSUME

"Your second lesson here in Frontier Town is: *Never assume you understand something.*[6] Don't rely on your human logic or the familiar, recognizable nature of things.[7] My army of end-time warriors is not chosen for their human abilities, status or past spiritual accomplishments. Those I am drawing by My Spirit to Frontier Town will have a different set of qualifications. Promotion comes from Me. I promote one and demote another. I choose whom I will. My training contradicts the world's standards. You will soon learn what I mean by this.

"Now, look at your manual, son," Jesus said. "I will give you the spiritual key to understanding and using it. Just like everything else here, it is not as it first appears."

I removed the manual from my shepherd's bag and held it in my hand. "Open it to the Table of Contents!" He instructed. "Yesterday, we walked the street of Frontier Town in the same order as you entered it today on Spirit Wind. You are troubled because he brought you to what you think is the end of the street. Actually, My Spirit led you to what is really the beginning of the street. We are standing in front of the first place where you must begin your training.

"The Table of Contents in your manual must be read by starting at the bottom first. The proper sequence in the *Field Manual for Spiritual Pioneers* begins at the bottom, not the top.[8] **The end is really the beginning.** This manual is to be read and understood from the end foreword. The site appearing last in your Table of Contents is the first one you must examine."

"This is amazing!" I said in total surprise. "The manual reads backwards, exactly the opposite of English, bottom to top instead of top to bottom, back to front instead of front to back." My eyes scanned down the column of symbolic, pictorial chapter headings finally coming to rest at the bottom of the page. Suddenly, it all made sense to me. Yesterday's trip down Main Street was a journey back to the beginning, but I didn't know it then. Now I realized that I had perceived it all backwards.

"You're amazing, Lord!" I declared. "This is implausible!"

He who has eyes, let him see, I thought. *Truly, the Lord causes the eyes of the proud to be closed, but He opens the eyes of the childlike. I must always start at the bottom; go first to the lowest place! This is where revelation knowledge begins. He gives grace to the humble.*[9]

GOD'S CHOICE

I quickly grasped the golden writing instrument and drew the outline of a key on the lower right corner of the Table of Contents. Inside the outline along the key's shaft I penned the words, "The last shall be first." Directly underneath them, I wrote, "Always begin at the bottom."

The feel of the pen scrolling across the page stirred a Samuel anointing within me. It was like tuning a radio receiver to improve the signal reception; revelation and prophetic discernment were activated in my spirit.

This has to be what Jesus felt when He spent the entire night in prayer before He selected the twelve apostles of the Lamb, I assumed. How vital it is to tune in to the Father's will and receive the unquestioning wisdom of the Almighty. Jesus selected His disciples with clear guidance from the Holy Spirit. He acted confidently because of this, choosing according to His Father's will and sovereign plan instead of His own.

Who can question His wisdom? I thought. Who would dare to invalidate His choice? This is the reason Samuel persevered until David arrived. It is this divine awareness that causes His prophets to see as God sees, not as men see.

SPIRITUAL BIGOTRY

My thoughts inevitably led me to the place of conviction. "Lord, I'm guilty of spiritual bigotry," I admitted. "I confess my fleshly tendency to categorize those around me as fit or unfit, qualified or unqualified for Your use."

I felt like Ananias who questioned God's wisdom when God asked him to go and pray for Saul of Tarsus. Everything in him resisted God's choice.[10] Ananias feared for his life. How could it be that God would take this evil persecutor of Christians and use him to reach the world with the gospel of the Kingdom? History proves that God knew exactly what He was doing!

"I must not catalog my brothers and sisters into classes of worthiness or spiritual maturity and giftedness," I said. "You must choose, Lord. You will decide who will be used as end-time warriors, not me.

"Forgive me, Lord," I prayed. "Help me to see others differently. You call many, but few are chosen.[11] From now on I must rely on Your insight. I need to seek Your direction. You know who Your spiritual pioneers are, Lord."

ONE MORE SURPRISE

I lifted my eyes from the pages of the manual and looked into Jesus' face. A definitive peace settled into my spirit. The confusion that began when we arrived at the end of Main Street and kept right on going was totally resolved. My spiritual world was turned right-side up. Now my perspective of Frontier Town was set in proper order.

I looked at Jesus with expectancy, indicating my eagerness to get started. "I think I'm ready, Lord!" I said. It was both a statement and a question.

"Then let's go, partner!" He replied, turning toward the boardwalk in front of the Log House.

What's inside the log structure? I wondered, striding boldly toward the edifice. To my consternation, Jesus turned abruptly to the left and headed for the pile of lumber lying in disarray on the ground adjacent to the building.

Caught totally by surprise, I couldn't silence my frustration. "Here I go again, Lord," I mumbled in dismay. "I am so led by presumption. **What can possibly be so important about a pile of lumber?" I asked.**

"Trust me, son. You are about to find out!"

VITAL LESSONS

The vision of Main Street gradually faded and I found myself standing near the opening of The Well of His Presence. Pondering what I had just seen and heard, the Spirit impressed me to make a notation in the field manual. Placing the book on the stone ledge of the well, I turned the pages to make the entry on the blank page opposite the Table of Contents.

My entry read: "*First Lesson*: Always be led by the Spirit. Your human wisdom and abilities will not suffice in Frontier Town. *Second Lesson*: Never assume you understand something. Don't be fooled by first impressions. And don't forget, you must learn to respect those whom God promotes. Things are not what they appear to be in Frontier Town. A spiritual pioneer must see things from God's perspective, not from man's viewpoint."

When I closed the book, the well faded from view.

Chapter Six

THE CONSTRUCTION SITE

Asignificant snowstorm, the first of the season, covered the New England landscape like a heavenly frosting of white icing on a chocolate cake. It was late morning when our plowman finally whooshed by the garage with his young son riding shotgun.

Smart man, I thought, waving a friendly and very grateful greeting as he ground to a stop. *Thank God he's got a copilot. He's probably been up all night; someone needs to keep him awake.*

He opened the window and peered down at me from his lofty perch. His red face and bulging, watery eyes were conspicuous behind the fur collar of his quilted, tan parka. "We'll take good care of you, pastor," he said, acting like Santa Claus with a plow on his sleigh. "I should have you all cleared up in about an hour." With that, his window abruptly closed and they disappeared in cloud of white powder.

Scurrying into the warm confines of my toasty study, I opened my journal with eager anticipation. *What does God have in store today in Frontier Town?* I thought, imagining yesterday's scene on Main Street. The vision came alive again as the Spirit ushered me into God's presence.

SURPRISING FAMILIARITY

Mannor greeted me with a disgruntled shove. "We've been waiting all morning for you," he said, pushing me toward the construction site.

A well deserved wake-up call, I thought sheepishly. *A lot has happened since yesterday. It's taken me all morning to get to The Secret Place. My spiritual senses need to be reactivated.*

The instant we stepped onto the building lot beyond the end of Main Street I became spellbound. I squinted in concentration, bewildered by my unanticipated sense of acquaintance with this plot of ground. Deep furrows of suspicion crept across my forehead.

> *The awesome presence of God suddenly supercharged the atmosphere.*

"Lord, this construction site has a strange familiarity about it," I said, touching Jesus' shoulder like a confused student appealing to his teacher. "I think I've been here before. I'm not sure what this means. I'm flabbergasted, Lord," I continued, awkwardly scrutinizing the scene. "Things are so different than what I thought I saw when I first viewed this building site."

KINGDOM STANDARDS REQUIRED

"Look!" I shouted with childlike wonder, pointing to the ground. "The surveyor's stakes are glowing!" Sparkling light radiated from the three gold pins. In an explosion of revelation, I suddenly realized what I was seeing.

"Jesus!" I gasped in shocked surprise. **"These pins, they're the surveyor's stakes of the Kingdom of God!** They are the same gold surveyor's pins that You revealed to me months ago in *The Hidden Kingdom*."[1]

The awesome presence of God suddenly supercharged the atmosphere. What I thought was just an empty lot and some building materials instantly became holy ground. Everything within me wanted to kneel and worship Him. Awestruck, I fell at Jesus' feet in the dust, pressed down by His glory.

"This is Your worksite, Lord," I uttered. "You're the One building something here of incredible value and eternal significance. This is sacred ground! These surveyor's pins were put here by Your sovereign will to identify the placement and dimensions of a very special project."

THE BUILDING INSPECTOR

I watched in wonder as Jesus approached the first surveyor's stake. With a humility that exemplifies authentic, genuine servanthood, He leaned over to touch the diamond on its top surface with his forefinger. The moment He did so, I felt a sudden, excruciating pain in my chest as though I had been stabbed with a knife. The stark reality of the vivid scene on the isolated beach in *The Hidden Kingdom* flashed into my memory.[2] I shivered with horror as the panorama of His crucifixion replayed on the screen of my mind. I was reliving the experience. "I drove this pin!" I groaned in anguish. "I hammered it into the ground. I'm the guilty one, Lord."

"You did it for me," I whispered, gasping for breath, barely able to express my overwhelming gratitude. "You died for me!" My eyes drowned in tears of gratitude. I cupped my face in my hands, fell face-down in the dust of the construction site and wept unashamedly until my tears were spent. Finally, my emotions somewhat recovered, I lifted my eyes toward the Master.

Jesus nodded his affirmation, but was undeterred. Without hesitation, He continued His inspection of the construction site. He ran his finger carefully along the taut cord stretched between the first and second surveyor's stakes. Suspended a foot above the ground, the cord ran parallel to the surface in a direct, level course about twenty-five feet toward the back of the lot. I watched intently as He traced its path with His finger. After pausing several times to ascertain that there were no snags or imperfections in the line, He arrived at the second pin. **The octagonal marker was driven securely into the soil at the precise spot predestined by God.**

IT'S ON FIRE!

"This pin is driven deeper than the first one," He said. "It is the Foundation Stake."[3]

"It's on fire, Lord!" I shouted, as the surveyor's pin burst into flame. "The top of it is burning!"

The pin was blazing like a torch buried upright in the ground. Tongues of holy fire danced upon its top, casting a crimson sheen on each of the six faces of the metallic marker. The words engraved on each face were clearly visible. "Repentance, Faith, Baptisms, The Laying on of Hands, Resurrection, Eternal Judgment," I recited, recalling from memory the three unseen faces that lay on the opposite side of the surveyor's stake, hidden from my view.[4]

Jesus paused for a long time to examine the second boundary marker. He peered down at it with the skill of a master craftsman ascertaining that it was set perfectly straight. He examined each face, searching for flaws or inaccuracies of any kind. When He was completely satisfied, He lifted His eyes heavenward and said softly, "It is well set, Father. Now we can proceed."

The word *proceed* had a catalytic effect upon me, creating a distinct awareness of commencement. Spiritual confidence flooded into me. I felt the uninhibited eagerness of a student when graduation finally arrives. I had successfully completed the required course of study. The approbation of my teachers was confirmed and I was granted permission to proceed to a new dimension of unlimited freedom, opportunity and accomplishment; this was only the beginning.

THE CRIMSON CORD

The cord wound around the flaming stake in a counterclockwise direction and then made a ninety-degree turn along the outside perimeter of the surveyor's pin. It departed toward the third marker from the face that read, "The Laying on of Hands." *This must be significant,* I thought. *God pays careful attention to even the slightest detail.*

Jesus proceeded to trace His finger along the cotton twine leading to the third surveyor's pin. I suddenly detected something about the cord I hadn't noticed at first glance. My eyes moved rapidly along the length of the strand back toward the second pin and then past it toward its origin point, carefully noting every detail.

"There are three strands," I whispered. The center of the twine was pure white cotton. Twisted around this central core was a blood-red thread running the entire length of the string. The third strand was a filament of gold filigree glistening its way along the length of the twine, encircling it with a sparkling reflection of holiness readily visible to the careful observer.

I turned my attention back to Jesus just as He reached the third surveyor's pin. He moved His hand gracefully above its mirrored surface in a royal blessing. Looking up into the western sky over Frontier Town, He began to pray. "Thank You, Father. From the first to the last, they have done well." His face bore the pleased look of a father boasting about his children who had performed exceptionally well. There was genuine pride in His voice.

THE BUILDERS' CODE

I stared in bewilderment as the third surveyor's pin began to flash on and off like an illuminated, electric signpost. This third Kingdom surveyor's stake consisted of five sides representing the five-fold ministries of the apostle, prophet, evangelist, pastor and teacher. What surprised me most was that only two of the segments were pulsating, the apostle and the prophet.[5]

Every time each face flashed it evoked an immediate response in my spirit. Intermittent power surges pulsed through my being as if an electrical switch were turned on and off inside of me. *Why am I responding to this signal so powerfully?* I wondered. *My spirit is bearing witness to these specific ministries.*

WHAT IS THIS PLACE?

I stood to my feet and slowly surveyed the supernatural building site. Everything was energized with spiritual life and power. It left me with more questions than answers. *What is this place? And why are there only three surveyor's pins? A normal building foundation usually has four. Where's the last pin? The string ends here at the third stake and there appears to be no string left.*

Then I remembered one of the most important lessons here in Frontier Town: *Things are not what they appear to be!*

Chapter Seven

A WORK IN PROGRESS

Jesus turned from the third surveyor's pin and walked directly to the untidy stack of lumber flung haphazardly into the center of the building site. He began to shift and sort through the boards to uncover those underneath the pile. His hands moved along the fine wood with a carpenter's ease. He studied the grain of each board with seasoned expertise, handling each piece as though He had hand-fashioned it Himself.

WHAT KIND OF WOOD IS THIS?

One newly uncovered board drew His attention. He raised it to His nose and drew a deep breath, savoring its north wood's sweetness as if it were incense. The unleashed aroma quickly dispersed into the construction site. I breathed deeply, drawing its revitalizing pungency fully into my lungs. Its concentrated essence was invigorating. **With a single breath, I felt life-giving strength surging into my body.**

I edged closer to the lumber pile, all the while marveling at the plank in His hands. "What type of wood is this?" I asked, looking down at the pile in amazement. "Every board is absolutely straight. Not a single one is warped or bowed. I can't see any knots either, Lord; and the grain – it's exquisite, so intricately detailed. The surface is so smooth that no sanding or polishing is required."

Jesus did not reply. Instead, He set the board down at my feet with no further instructions and continued to arrange the lumber pile. I reached down to pick up the single plank. It was so heavy I had to tighten my grip so that I wouldn't drop it. The rich purplish-brown color gave it a very old, well oiled appearance. "This isn't freshly cut," I stated. "This board must be fashioned from an ancient, virgin forest. I've never seen such beautiful wood in my life."

An unexpected covetousness overcame me. I clenched the board in my hands. "I want this wood for myself," I said, like a selfish, demanding child, not caring that Jesus saw my unrestrained lust for the wood. "Something inside me can only be fulfilled by possessing these boards," I said, looking at Jesus without apology.

I rested one end of the board on the ground. Forming a fist with my right hand, I struck the flat surface with my knuckles. "This is the hardest wood I've ever seen. It's indestructible. No force can change it or harm it. "What is it?" I pondered, turning the board to examine the opposite side.

THE MANUFACTURER'S ID

Before my very eyes, burned into the face of the wood in large charred letters, was an identification mark. The manufacturer had stamped this piece, clearly distinguishing it from all the others. The inscription was a location in the Bible: *Psalm 139.* The text instantly flashed into my mind. I could even recall the heading: "God's Perfect Knowledge of Man."

Standing in the middle of the construction site of Main Street, lumber in hand, I quoted the Scripture. *"O Lord, You have searched me and known me. You know my sitting down and my rising up; You understand my thought afar off. You comprehend my path and my lying down, and are acquainted with all my ways"* (Psalm 139:1-3).

I paused to look at Jesus. He was listening to every word and watching me with supernatural discernment. *He knows that this is one of my favorite Psalms,* I thought.

Looking into His eyes with childlike transparency, I continued, *"For there is not a word on my tongue, but behold, O Lord, You know it altogether. You have hedged me behind and before, and laid Your hand upon me. Such knowledge is too wonderful for me; It is high, I cannot attain it.*

"Where can I go from Your Spirit? Or where can I flee from Your presence? If I ascend into heaven, You are there; if I make my bed in hell, behold, You are there. If I take the wings of the morning, and dwell in the uttermost parts of the sea, even there Your hand shall lead me, and Your right hand shall hold me. If I say, 'Surely the darkness shall fall on me,' Even the night shall be light about me. Indeed, the darkness shall not hide from You, But the night shines as the day. The darkness and the light are both alike to You" (Psalm 139:4-12).

"These words are absolutely true, Lord!" I said. "I think I know now what David meant when he wrote them. I'm experiencing it right now here in Your presence, Jesus. You truly are all-knowing and inescapable."

PROCESSED IN THE SECRET PLACE

I continued to quote David's words as if they were my own. *"For You formed my inward parts; You covered me in my mother's womb. I will praise You, for I am fearfully and wonderfully made; Marvelous are Your works, and that my soul knows very well. My frame was not hidden from You, when I was made in secret, and skillfully wrought in the lowest parts of the earth"* (Psalm 139:13-15).

Sudden revelation exploded inside of me. "Lord, You formed me *in the Secret Place*! The Secret Place," I repeated, processing the spiritual significance of the words.

"The Secret Place is like a spiritual womb where you shape and mold each person. The Secret Place is real; it exists deep within us. It's where our spiritual formation takes place," I said.

"Yes," Jesus replied. "That's how much I love everyone. I am intimately involved in forming and shaping each individual life."

"Your eyes saw my substance, being yet unformed," I continued, *"and in Your book they all were written, the days fashioned for me, when as yet there were none of them. How precious also are Your thoughts to me, O God! How great is the sum of them! If I should count them, they would be more in number than the sand; When I awake, I am still with You"* (Psalm 39:16-18).

THE BUILDERS' SEAL OF APPROVAL

My tears splashed onto the deep rose-colored wooden beam as I bowed my head in His presence and began to pray with total abandonment. *"Search me, O God, and know my heart; Try me, and know my anxieties; and see if there is any wicked way in me; and lead me in the way everlasting"* (Psalm139:23-24).

After a moment, He spoke. "It's all right, son," He said. "I know your heart better than you do. Your life is an open book to Me."

I lifted my head to look at the amazing stack of lumber before me. "Is each piece like this one, Jesus?" I asked.

"Yes," He replied. "Go ahead, son," He encouraged. "Search through the pile."

EXAMINING THE WORD

I lifted the boards one by one, searching for the wood-burned inscriptions. The markings changed in script style from board to board. Each impression was unique, identifying the craftsman who had fashioned the priceless wood at the Lord's bidding. Each piece of lumber varied in length, width and thickness.

This is like having my own personal, Spirit-led Bible study, I thought, eagerly lifting the planks of finely crafted wood. I handled each one with the ease that comes from familiarity. I had studied them many times before in real life. Some of the boards were so familiar to me that I immediately recognized the intricate grain patterns and paused to admire the well-worked, smooth surface of the wood. With each successive plank, an incredible chronology of texts began to unfold.

THE MAIN BEAM

Matthew 16 appeared on one of the boards. It radiated with prophetic truth. "This must be the main beam," I said, shifting its heavy weight in my hands while quoting the text.

"Who do men say that I, the Son of Man, am?" So they said, "Some say John the Baptist, some Elijah, and others, Jeremiah or one of the prophets."

He said to them, "But who do you say that I am?" Simon Peter answered and said, "You are the Christ, the Son of the Living God."

Matthew 16:13-16

"This timber has such solid strength about it that it can easily support any weight or resist any stress applied to it!" I declared with confidence. "Its thick, square, beam-like sides are the epitome of enduring strength."

When I dropped the heavy board to the hardened earth, the crashing sound of the beam striking the ground exploded above the building site and sped down the street of Frontier Town, penetrating far beyond it into the boundless plain and the unseen distance. *Absolute, limitless, eternal truth*, I thought as the sound faded into eternity.

CHOSEN, BUT NOT YET PERFECT

The moment I lifted the next plank from the pile, Jesus stepped forward and slid His hand along its surface in one continuous motion to check for roughness and splinters.

The yellow pine plank, freshly drawn from the bottom of the pile, was softer than the others. I was immediately chagrinned by the anomalous, disfiguring knots along its length. Oddly, they appeared to be quite acceptable to the Lord. In fact, He gave special attention to each knot, examining its uniqueness with an appreciation for its particular characteristics.

The manufacturer's mark was burned into the far edge of the surface: *Ephesians 4:11-13.*

And He Himself gave some to be apostles, some prophets, some evangelists, and some pastors and teachers, for the equipping of the saints for the work of ministry, for the edifying of the body of Christ, till we all come to the unity of the faith and of the knowledge of the Son of God, to a perfect [mature] man, to the measure of the stature of the fullness of Christ.

Ephesians 4:11-13

"That explains it," I said. **"Now I understand why these knots are acceptable to You, Lord. You use imperfect people to accomplish Your purpose.** This

55

plank is cut from a much larger piece," I observed, noticing saw marks on the end of the plank. "You are still supplying us with the ministry we need to grow up into mature Christians."

THE CONSTRUCTION CREW

I placed the board back on the ground next to *Psalm 139* and *Matthew 16*. When I stood up, an unexplained sense of *déjà vu* came over me. "There's something about these three boards, Lord," I said. "I recognize their order. And this last one, there's something very significant about it that I am not getting. What is it?" I asked, searching the pile of lumber for an answer.

In response to my question, Jesus turned away from the lumber pile and pointed deliberately at the third surveyor's stake protruding from the hard ground of the building site. "Out of the mouth of two or three witnesses, a thing is established," He said.

I suddenly realized the obvious connection between the third surveyor's pin and the last lumber plank at my feet. "Okay, Lord. I see the similarity," I said, quizzically, "but why is this important? Apostles, prophets, evangelist, pastors and teachers," I pondered. Then it hit me.

"Of course! They're the certified and approved builders here in Frontier Town. God uses the hands of real people. They are His trained and anointed craftsman, Spirit-led men and women who shape and construct the lives of every one of His children into a mature, spiritual house of faith."

A FULL DAY'S WORK

"Your work here is not finished," the Lord said, pointing toward the untidy pile of wood. "There are a few more pieces in this pile that are critical to your training in Frontier Town. You must examine them before we can move on."

Chapter Eight

HOME, SWEET HOME

I felt like a student about to enter Bible College, eager to learn but sobered by the responsibility of attained knowledge. "Ignorance may be bliss, but it can also kill you," I said, bending over the lumber pile with renewed concentration. "Today is not some sort of rehearsal for tomorrow. The things I'm learning here in Frontier Town are critical. I had better learn my lessons well."

"Guide me, Holy Spirit," I prayed, as I chose another piece of wood. When I lifted the small rectangular board, its weight pressed upon my spirit. It looked like a spindle for a porch railing. Stamped on the blunt end of the short piece in small burned letters was the text, *Genesis 29:1-11*. It flashed into my mind with obvious familiarity. God had indelibly written this passage upon my heart years ago when I was a greenhorn pastor.

WATER THE SHEEP

"Jacob set out again on his way to the people of the east. He noticed a well out in an open field with three flocks of sheep bedded down around it. This was the common well from which the flocks were watered. The stone over the mouth of the well was huge. When all the flocks were gathered, the shepherds would roll the stone from the well and water the sheep; then they would return the stone, covering the well.

Jacob said, "Hello friends. Where are you from?"

They said, "We're from Haran."

Jacob asked, "Do you know Laban son of Nahor?"

"We do."

"Are things well with him?" Jacob continued.

"Very well," they said. "And here is his daughter Rachel coming with the flock."

Jacob said, "There's a lot of daylight still left; it isn't time to round up the sheep yet, is it? So why not water the flocks and go back to grazing?"

"We can't," they said. "Not until all the shepherds get here. It takes all of us to roll the stone from the well. Not until then can we water the flocks."

While Jacob was in conversation with them, Rachel came up with her father's sheep. She was the shepherd. The moment Jacob saw Rachel, daughter of Laban his mother's brother, saw her arriving with his uncle Laban's sheep, he went and single-handedly rolled the stone from the mouth of the well and watered the sheep of his uncle Laban. Then he kissed Rachel and broke into tears."

Genesis 29:1-11, MSG

MADE FOR INTIMACY

I stared at the piece of wood in my hand, considering that it might be the most valuable in the entire world. "Jacob's well," I said. "It's just like The Well of Your Presence. **Nothing in this world can ever assuage my spiritual thirst except a drink from Your well of intimacy, Jesus.**"

Memories of the hours and days I have spent in The Well of His Presence scrolled through my mind like the filled pages of my journals: the sudden discovery of intimacy with God in *The Secret Place;* the privilege of sweet communion and conversation with God in The Well of His Presence; the wonder and delight of plumbing the incredible depths of mystery, revelation and creativity in *The Hidden Kingdom;* walking with Jesus and my newfound angelic companions in the Spirit; exploring the spiritual landscape just as Enoch walked with God; and above all, the life-giving, life-sustaining fulfillment of simply being with Jesus. My cup was overflowing.

THE BRIDE AT THE WELL

"Just like Jacob did, Lord, You have single-handedly removed the stone of hindrance that keeps us from intimacy with You," I said. "You draw us into Your presence with the passion of a Bridegroom yearning for His bride. When we respond to Your invitation, You lovingly care for our needs just like Jacob cared for Rachel's sheep. When we drink from Your well, our presence fulfills Your longing for intimacy with us. You kiss us and weep with joy.[1] You don't care who knows or sees. Your love is shameless."

"I am created for intimacy with You, Jesus," I continued, gazing into His face with a manly tenderness and affection. "It doesn't surprise me that Rachel first found intimacy with Jacob at the well. Just like Rachael, I long to get to The Well of Your Presence."

You draw us into Your presence with the passion of a Bridegroom yearning for His bride.

SHAMELESS LOVE

Jesus' face was glowing with utter joy. Huge tears dripped down His cheeks. He lifted His arms toward me. I rushed into His embrace. Like Jacob and Rachael, the bride and the bridegroom, we stood weeping together in each other's arms in the middle of the construction site on Main Street in Frontier Town. Our love was genuine, pure and unashamed.

When He finally withdrew, satisfaction pervaded every cell of my being. "I love you, Jesus," I said. "I feel like I'm home!"

"You are!" He replied.

AN URGENT PROPHECY!

I turned back to the stack of lumber with the confidence of a son who knows he is loved. An unexpected, immediate sense of prophetic urgency gripped my soul. "What are You trying to say to me, Holy Spirit?" I prayed. **"Is there an urgent prophetic word for Your church that needs to be released from The Well of Your Presence?"**

SPIRIT WIND

EARTHQUAKE IN FRONTIER TOWN

I extracted the next board with determination, twisting it free from the bottom of the pile. My hands burned as though I had grasped a hot iron. Hebrews 12:25-29 leapt into my spirit before I even saw the inscription on the surface of the wood. The words trumpeted from the throne room of God with blazing judgment and absolute authority.

See that you do not refuse Him who speaks. For if they did not escape who refused Him who spoke on earth, much more shall we not escape if we turn away from Him who speaks from heaven, whose voice then shook the earth; but now He has promised, saying, "Yet once more I shake not only the earth, but also heaven."

Now this, "Yet once more," indicates the removal of those things that are being shaken, as of things that are made, that the things which cannot be shaken may remain.

Therefore, since we are receiving a kingdom which cannot be shaken, let us have grace, by which we may serve God acceptably with reverence and godly fear. For our God is a consuming fire.

Hebrews 12: 25-29

I jumped back in sudden fear. "It's about the end times," I gasped.

The ground shook violently under my feet. Even the angels quivered as the earthquake rumbled through Frontier Town.

"This tremor is a prophetic sign of the real and prolonged shaking that has begun on the earth and in the heavens," Jesus said.

THERE IS HOPE

"Lord, help me to remain standing," I pleaded in holy fear, desperately searching for something to steady me. I lunged at a dusty, antiquated piece of wood lying at my feet, hoping that it would provide some stability. The board was carved and embellished. It looked like a piece of decorative trim taken from an old building. It could have been used to beautify an abandoned temple. It was obvious to me that someone had discarded it, but God had retrieved and restored it.

An inscription was burned deep into the wood by the Holy Spirit, an ancient promise from centuries past. I was holding the final text of the prophetic message in my hands.

"For behold, the day is coming, burning like an oven, and all the proud, yes, all who do wickedly will be stubble. And the day which is coming shall burn them up," says the Lord of hosts, "That will leave them neither root nor branch.

"But to you who fear My name the Sun of Righteousness shall arise with healing in His wings… Behold, I will send you Elijah the prophet before the coming of the great and dreadful day of the Lord. And he will turn the hearts of the fathers to the children, and the hearts of the children to their fathers, lest I come and strike the earth with a curse"

Malachi 4: 1-2, 5-6

"Is there still hope for us, Lord?" I asked in desperation.

"Yes," He replied, "there is hope."

THE FINAL FRONTIER

Jesus immediately retrieved two boards from the remaining pile and laid them at my feet in proper order. "These are the last two," He said.

I lifted the first one to eye level. The inscription was branded into the center of the plank: *Joshua 1:10-11.*

Then Joshua commanded the officers of the people, saying, "Pass through the camp and command the people, saying 'Prepare provisions for yourselves, for within three days you will cross over this Jordan, to go in to possess the land which the Lord your God is giving you to possess.' "

Joshua 1:10-11

"The Joshua generation is My answer," He said. "I am preparing a Joshua generation to possess the final frontier. Their prophetic voice will be lifted to the ends of the earth. Every nation, tribe and tongue will hear the gospel of the Kingdom. They are My end-time warriors."

61

Although no one was visibly present in Frontier Town, I peered optimistically down the street. "There must be thousands of end-time warriors here just like me, Lord," I said. "I just can't see them. There have got to be more Christians who have been drawn here by the Holy Spirit for training and equipping."

The courage of God rose up within me. It wasn't youthful innocence, carelessness or presumption; it was the resolute response of someone who has wandered long enough in the wilderness of religious hypocrisy and the emptiness of unfulfilled hopes and visions to be thoroughly disillusioned with church as usual.

"We must take the land!" I shouted in determined frustration. "We can do it with Your help, Lord. We dare not turn back to wander in the spiritual wilderness wasting the lives of another generation. We've got to stop playing religious games that keep us going in circles, merely retracing our steps. The fullness of time has come. This is the hour! We must take possession of the final frontier!"

I spoke with youthful vigor and determined resolve. "This must be how Caleb felt. Give me the high ground!" I shouted, turning toward Jesus. But He was gone.

TOTAL VICTORY

Blazing light suddenly illuminated the building site. It radiated from a single, blinding source above my head. I squinted in an attempt to examine it. Something was spinning at supersonic speed in the center of the brilliance.

"It's the fourth surveyor's pin," I uttered in amazement.[2] The effulgence of God's glory shimmered from the three-sided pin like a million suns. The fullness of God's awesome glory and presence, Father, Son and Holy Spirit, saturated everything. Awestruck, I shielded my eyes in an attempt to watch the surveyor's pin slowly rise heavenward. It continued upward until it was no longer visible. Its light dispersed through Frontier Town and slowly dissolved into a cloud of luminous fog.

A deafening clap of thunder suddenly shattered the air like the roar of an attacking lion. It growled over Frontier Town, frightening me to the core. I froze in place, afraid to move even a muscle. **The flash of a single bolt of lightning discharged from the center of the cloud and struck the last remaining**

board at my feet. A wisp of black smoke rose from the charred surface, filling the air with the pungent smell of burned wood

I reached for the still-smoking plank with trembling, awestruck fear. Red embers sparkled and smoldered where the inscription was burned into the surface. The charred letters read *First Corinthians 15.* The verses instantly appeared, suspended in the atmosphere in front of me. The Holy Spirit wrote them in the air as if it were an acetate transparency.

> *But now Christ is risen from the dead, and has become the firstfruits of those who have fallen asleep. For since by man came death, by Man also came the resurrection of the dead. For as in Adam all die, even so in Christ all shall be made alive.*
>
> *But each one in his own order: Christ the firsfruits, afterward those who are Christ's at His coming. Then comes the end, when He delivers the Kingdom to God the Father, when He puts an end to all rule and all authority and power. For He must reign until He has put all enemies under His feet. The last enemy that will be destroyed is death. … Now when all things are made subject to Him, then the Son Himself will also be subject to Him who put all things under Him, that God may be all in all.*

First Corinthians 15: 20-26, 28

GOD BUILDS PEOPLE

I turned to survey the construction site one last time. "Surely this is a supernatural work in progress," I said, standing alone in the center of the lot. I had no sooner uttered the words, than I felt as though I were abruptly awakened from a sound sleep. The realization of where I was hit me.

"This is my life!" I blurted out. "This construction site is me! These surveyors' stakes, they're driven into the spiritual core of my being. God set them in place by His own hand," I said, clutching my chest.

I bent over to hold the white cord between my fingers. "This cord is the righteousness of Jesus; the crimson thread is His blood shed for my sins. The gold thread identifies me as a royal heir of the King of kings."

THE CONCORDANCE OF MY LIFE

"And the lumber," I said, observing the planks with appreciation. "Every one of these Scriptures is part of my life. They're more than scattered bits of truth carelessly tossed here. God chose them to shape my life. They are timbers of truth harvested by the Holy Spirit from God's Word and assembled in my heart by the hand of God, life texts that have determined my spiritual destiny. God has established their truth in my life, line upon line."

"This is my life," I said with humility. "God is working on me, right here on Main Street where everyone can see the progress. That's why we had to start here. He's been working on me for a long time. I'm a work in progress."

A BUILDING PLAN

The mystery of the construction site was solved. I stepped back onto the street. To my surprise, stretching off into the distance leading out of Frontier Town were hundreds of similar sites at various stages of construction, each one containing three surveyor's pins and a stack of lumber.

"I'm not the only one God is working on. This is a massive Kingdom development," I said, in gratitude. "He is establishing His Kingdom principles in every one of His children. God's Word is the lumber of life. There's an entire army of end-time warriors assembled right here in Frontier Town. I don't know why I didn't see them before.

"If any of you can hear my voice," I shouted, "I'm sure if you look carefully, you will find the construction site that belongs to you. You're a part of the Joshua generation!"

Tired from the hard day's work, I mounted Spirit Wind and rode out of town. *"Things truly are not what they seem to be in Frontier Town,"* I mused.

Spirit Wind lowered his head and sped across the plain toward the sunset like the wind. I'm not sure how long we rode through the darkness. Sleep came somewhere along the way.

Chapter Nine

THE DOORWAY TO DESTINY

I was awakened by the penetrating chill of the desert morning. The sun provided little heat, and I shivered as I remounted Spirit Wind. I fixed my eyes on the distant horizon with inquisitive eagerness. Somewhere far across this barren plain Frontier Town was waking to a new day. *Spirit Wind knows where we're going,* I reassured myself, settling back in the saddle for the long ride ahead.

Spirit Wind trotted across the open prairie, swaying effortlessly back and forth. *I want to savor this moment as long as possible,* I thought. *There's something about riding this majestic horse. He moves with such ease.*

The suede shepherd's bag brushed rhythmically against my thigh like a metronome synchronized to Spirit Wind's pace. I tugged on the drawstring to assure the safety of its contents. My thoughts flashed back to the moment when Jesus had first given me this special container.

Everything I need for my spiritual journey is safely stored in this pouch, I thought, *including My newly acquired golden writing instrument and my personal copy of* The Field Manual for Spiritual Pioneers.

A cold sense of dread suddenly swept over me. *Oh no! The Letter,* I thought. *I haven't seen it.* I squeezed the bag, groping with anxious urgency to feel for the stiff parchment letter that Jesus had given me.[1] *Surely I haven't lost it.*

I breathed a huge sigh of relief as I felt the faint outline of the priceless letter inside the bag. "I know every word of it is written on my heart," I said to

Spirit Wind, "but if I should ever need it to prove my identity, just having it in my heart won't be very convincing."

THE STARS' SONG

It was late in the evening when Spirit Wind and I passed the houses and buildings of Frontier Town and came to a gentle stop at the hitching post at the end of Main Street. The white stallion shook his head back and forth, as horses do with satisfaction at the end of a long run, and exhaled his steamy breath

Stars really do sing!

with a "plplplplpl" to announce our arrival. His sparkling white mane rustled in the wind as he pawed in the dust with his right front hoof and bowed his head. Then he stood motionless, every muscle relaxed, as if to say, "We're here!"

The stars glistened like sparkling diamonds in the black desert sky overhead. I gazed into the heavens, overwhelmed by the celestial extravaganza. Every star shimmered as though it were sending a message to me in Morse code. "They're singing," I whispered in amazement. **Like musical notes, each one contributed to the heavenly symphony composed by God and scrolled across the cosmos.**[2]

I recalled, from some long forgotten science classroom, that sound can be carried upon light waves. We humans can only hear a very limited frequency range.

Stars really do sing! I thought. *We just can't hear them right now, but some day we will! Their shimmering, though unheard, declaration of the glory of God makes me want to worship.*

THE APPOINTED TIME

I could have sat gazing into the heavens for hours, but my reverie was interrupted by Jesus' arrival. He appeared on the wooden deck next to the door of the log cabin. "I have brought you here now, because your appointed time has arrived," He said, pointing at the door. "You must enter here," He instructed.

66

Dismounting Spirit Wind, I climbed the steps onto the wooden deck and obediently walked past the Lord toward the closed door. *What will I find inside and why do I have to enter here first?* I thought. I felt like an apprehensive recruit about to enter basic training, but excited about the challenge.

As I reached for the doorknob, out of the corner of my left eye I caught a glimpse of the sign hanging on the exterior wall. To my surprise, my name was printed in bold letters in the left column directly under the heading, "Arriving." The black ink was still wet. A series of mysterious stars appeared directly after my name.

That's intriguing! I thought. *I wonder if they represent some sort of celestial clock indicating that this is the appointed time chosen by God for me to enter this door. Not only can stars sing, they can also proclaim events, I considered. The birth of Jesus was announced by a star. God's ways are different than ours and His thoughts above ours!* [3] *We must learn to speak and understand His language of symbols and images.*

DESTINY AWAITS

I grasped the knob. Its icy coldness penetrated my flesh. I quickly turned it, thrust open the door, and stepped past the threshold into the interior of the log cabin. A sobering sense of divine purpose engulfed me. "This is a *kiaros* moment," I said. "This is the doorway to my destiny."

The cabin was dimly lit by some unseen source. A haze filled the room like a cloud of cigarette smoke. In the left rear corner several men were seated around a circular wooden table, leaning back on the rear legs of their tilted chairs in relaxed conversation.

There was an obvious camaraderie among the men. I could hear bits and pieces of the stories they were sharing with each other. They spoke of daring exploits and amazing encounters with danger and battle. They were well traveled and bore the traits of experienced men who had journeyed many miles. I knew they could share a wealth of wisdom with someone as inexperienced as I. *If only I had a chance to talk with them,* I thought. *I have so many questions about this place.*

IDENTIFICATION REQUIRED

I felt a sudden pull toward the figure of a man standing enshrouded in the haze to my right. He was partially hidden behind a podium-like counter. A large book, something like a registration book you would find in a swank hotel, lay open in front of him.

The mysterious figure was of average height. His face was masked in the shadows cast from the hood of the dull brown, ascetic robe covering his head. The scratchy wool material seemed extremely durable and well suited for a long, arduous journey. A white, braided-rope belt was tied around his waist.

As far as I can tell, for all intents and purposes, this guy is a monk! I thought. *He looks like one of the desert fathers from a far-distant time and place. My guess is that he's spent decades alone with God in the wilderness. But what's he doing here in Frontier Town? He sure is out of place here!*

I walked toward the counter with the wariness of a hunter stalking his prey. I stood before the table directly in front of him, not knowing what to expect or say. Fortunately, he broke the silence.

"Where are your credentials?" he asked in a gruff, demanding tone.

"My credentials?" I said, in confusion. "I have no credentials!"

My pulse raced anxiously. *What does he want?* I thought, perplexed by this unforeseen requirement. A shudder of apprehension and doubt swept over me. *What am I doing here?* I trembled, shaking my head back and forth in denial. *Why did I ever think I was qualified to begin this journey? What a miserable failure I am.*

I felt like a spiritual impostor trying to pass myself off as someone important to God. *I might as well quit now. It's all over. I'm doomed to failure. I'll never get past this first building,* I complained. I turned away from the counter with an aching sadness in my heart.

Is this it? Is this the end? I'll never know what Frontier Town is all about. What good will the Field Manual for Spiritual Pioneers *do me now?* Disappointment flooded over me in recurring waves of deferred hope and vanquished dreams. I was heartbroken.

I reached into my leather pouch to retrieve the field manual. "I'll return it to Jesus when I get outside. He can give it to someone else," I thought. My hand accidentally brushed past the parchment letter Jesus had given me months ago. My spirit ignited with a glimmer of hope.

AUTHENTICITY

Spinning around in my tracks, I rushed back to the raised podium holding the document in my outstretched hand. "Will this do?" I pleaded.

The hooded figure reached out to receive the folded document. The red ribbon lying across the face of the parchment and the royal blue and gold seal instantly caught his attention. He scrutinized the embossed design in the wax with expert knowledge like a jeweler looking through his eyeglass at a priceless gemstone.

He really is taking his time, I thought, trembling like a frightened alien citizen trying to cross the border illegally. *Apparently some folks have tried to enter Frontier Town with counterfeit credentials.*

He examined it for what seemed an eternity. When he was fully convinced of its authenticity he loosened the seal and opened the letter. I watched his eyes for any sign of acceptance as they moved down the single page of the document. His mouth formed the words as he read them: "Dale, Friend of God. One who walks with the Son," and then he came to the signature: "Signed, Jesus."

He raised his head, and smiled. "Welcome, Dale! I am blessed to receive you as a traveling companion," he said, in a reassuring, congenial tone. "Please sign here!"

"That was close!" I uttered, under my breath. "I'd never have gotten in without this letter of recommendation from Jesus."

He pointed to an empty space in the open ledger halfway down the right page. His forefinger rested on the vacant line. His hand was wrinkled with age. Short silver wisps of hair lay curled on the leathered skin. It was a fatherly type of hand, reassuring and comforting, but strong and work-toughened with thick calluses.

I breathed a sigh of relief as I searched the counter top for a pen. There was none to be found. "There's no pen, sir?" I asked.

"Yes, there is," he replied.

"Aha," I declared with relish. "I won't be fooled again." I confidently reached into my shepherd's bag to procure my writing instrument and signed my name in the appropriate space.

A SURPRISE INTRODUCTION

I returned the pen to my pouch. When I looked up the mysterious figure had lowered his hood, exposing his amicable face. He stretched forth his right hand in a gesture of friendship and introduced himself. "Welcome, Dale. My name is Abraham."

The moment our hands clasped I felt a kindred spirit with this ancient patriarch. *I'm in the presence of my spiritual father,* I gasped in delighted surprise. "I'm honored to meet you, Abraham," I said. "I'm just a young spiritual pioneer. I have so much to learn."

"I know," he smiled reassuringly. "And that's exactly why you have been summoned here by the Master."

He glanced momentarily at the table in the far corner where the mysterious men were eavesdropping on our conversation. "Let me explain the details of your enlistment," he continued.

THE PIONEER'S PLEDGE

Abraham lifted a wood plaque from a shelf under the podium and placed it on the counter. "Examine this carefully!" he said. A document was laminated onto the shiny wood surface. It appeared to be an official certificate that was permanently preserved for display purposes.

"This is the pledge of every spiritual pioneer," he explained, pointing to the words at the top of the document. "Every end-time warrior must agree to these demands. The requirements have not changed since they were formulated by the Lord when He first spoke them to me."

The ancient patriarch ran his rugged forefinger across the words with surprising youthfulness and then began to quote them aloud. His personal experience was reflected in every uttered word. Years of pilgrimage flashed across his wrinkled face like scenes from an ancient desert landscape as he retraced in his mind the trail of altars built, wells dug and tents pitched in his thirsty, relentless pursuit of the Living God. *"Now the Lord had said to Abram: Get out of your country, from your family and from your father's house, to a land that I will show you. I will make you a great nation; I will bless you and make your name great; and you shall be a blessing. I will bless those who bless you, and I will curse him who curses you; and in you all the families of the earth shall be blessed"* (Genesis 12:1-3).

Immediately below the pledge an official-looking diploma appeared, written in expert calligraphy. I read it with careful consideration.

"Now the Lord had said to Abram: 'Get out of your coun-
try, from your family and from your father's house, to a land
that I will show you. I will make you a great nation; I will
bless you and make your name great; and you shall be a
blessing. I will bless those who bless you, and I will curse
him who curses you; and in you all the families of the earth
shall be blessed' " (Genesis 12:1-3).

Certificate of Completion
In Recognition of Obedient Response to the Call of God
This is to certify that

_____

has successfully completed the primary course of

instruction for Spiritual Pioneers and is hereby

accorded the affirmation of his peers and mentors

and fully commissioned to possess the Land.

Signed on this day of our Lord , _____

At Frontier Town;

"Now the Lord had said to Abram,

'Get out of your country, from your family and from
your father's house, to a land that I will show you.' "

"Going on Still" (Genesis 12:9)

Several lines were left empty beneath the date for signatures. Another
Scripture appeared near the bottom of the document. *"Now the Lord had said*
to Abram, 'Get out of your country, from your family and from your father's house,
to a land that I will show you' " (Genesis 12:1) .

Three final words, perfectly centered at the bottom of the page, concluded the document. Their meaning and intent were sobering and encouraging.

They punctuated the diploma with the clear idea of unrelenting determination and persistence. They expressed the heart of every pioneer. *"Going on Still"* (Genesis 12:9).

FREEDOM TO CHOOSE

A gold chain framed the 8 ½ x 11 certificate. It was fastened to each corner with miniature nails the size of earring posts. These studs were inserted into holes that had been stabbed into the wood's surface by an awl.

The chain links were joined in an alternating fashion; one link was shaped in the outline of a heart, the next one adjacent to it a gold arrow with feathers and a pointed head. Each arrow had the word "Bond" engraved upon its shaft. Every heart had the word "Slave" inscribed on its surface. The arrows connected the hearts and held the chain together. **In one continuously repeating phrase, the chain read, "Bond-Slave-Bond-Slave-Bond-Slave."**

If this chain were not attached to the plaque, it would make a beautiful gold necklace, I thought, *but no clasp is present. It's seamless.* The chain's message reminded me of how the freed Hebrew slaves pierced their ears on their master's doorpost with an awl, freely choosing to become a bond slave, committing themselves to an entire lifetime of service.[4]

ARE YOU WILLING?

"Are you willing to make the pledge, son?" Abraham asked in a serious tone. His furrowed brow clearly communicated the gravity of the moment.

"Yes!" I replied, in total abandonment to God's will. "My heart is steadfast. I am absolutely certain, Abraham."

"Then place your hand here. We will pray." He pointed to the empty line in the center of the certificate.

I placed my palm directly over the blank space with determined resolve and bowed my head. A holy hush descended upon the room.

Abraham placed his weathered, calloused hand over mine. He prayed with unwavering faith. "Father," he said. "Your Kingdom come, your will be done, on earth as it is in heaven." He paused to reflect for a moment and then continued. "Thank you for this warrior, Lord, and for all those just like him that you have called here to Frontier Town. Give them spiritual eyes to see as You see. Grant them courage to overcome and the endurance to take the high ground."

He stroked the back of my hand with his thumb and then vowed with the seasoned experience of one who is a pioneer himself, "I will encourage him, Lord!"[5]

A SPIRITUAL COVENANT

I stood perfectly still for a long time. When I finally lifted my hand from the plaque I was dumbfounded. "My name," I whispered. "It's written on the line in my very own handwriting." I traced the signature with my forefinger. "This is amazing. I must have signed it in the Spirit."

"This certificate, was it prepared just for me?" I asked in astonishment, looking quizzically into Abraham's eyes.

"Yes," he replied. "You have agreed to accept the call of God upon your life. You have taken the pledge of a spiritual pioneer. You are now enlisted in God's army as an end-time warrior."

"How many more of these documents are stored beneath the desk?" I asked.

"I have enough for everyone God has called," he replied. "Many more will receive His invitation in the days ahead and thousands have already arrived before you. Each one is summoned here for training, just like you."

BAND OF BROTHERS

"Your time here is finished," Abraham said abruptly, like someone expecting the arrival of another appointment.

The sound of shuffling feet from the far corner sped across the room. Chairs banged to the floor and skidded under the circular wooden table as the men rose and pushed them into place. As if they were responding to some unheard command, all four men simultaneously headed for the door. Their boots thumped on the wood floor as they scuffed past me.

They were dressed in typical western plaid shirts. Wide leather belts held their Levis low around their waists. Their leather boots were beautifully worked and embossed. Each man had a different colored cowboy hat with a highly personalized shape to it. They lowered their heads, deliberately hiding their faces from view. Each one touched the brim of his hat as he passed in front of me to indicate an unspoken greeting. I barely heard one say, "Howdy, partner!" I had the distinct impression that I would meet him again somewhere in Frontier Town.

A BUSINESS CARD

"There's one more thing I must give you," Abraham said, opening the small cardboard box sitting to his right on the counter top. "Carry this with you at all times!" he instructed, handing me a business card. I fully expected it to be his. I was stunned by what I saw; my own name was printed in the upper left corner in red ink. On the upper, right corner, also in red ink, my title appeared: Spiritual Pioneer. **In the center of the card, in black ink, was a short quote from God's Word:** *"Searching for a city whose builder and maker is God."* Along the bottom of the card was the spiritual warrior's motto that I had first seen in the *Field Manual for Spiritual Pioneers*: "To Conquer, To Love, To Redeem."

I recognized the Scripture quote from Hebrews chapter eleven. Its context read: *"By faith Abraham obeyed when he was called to go out to the place which he would receive as an inheritance. And he went out, not knowing where he was going. By faith he dwelt in the land of promise as in a foreign country, dwelling in tents with Isaac and Jacob, the heirs with him of the same promise; for he waited for the city which has foundations, whose builder and maker is God"* (Hebrews 11: 8-10).

"Thank you, Abraham," I said, sincerely. "I will keep this with me at all times!" I turned to go.

THE REGISTRATION BOOK

"Wait!" Abraham demanded. "Please close the book before you leave."

I obediently reached to shut the registration book. Grasping it in both hands, my eyes scanned the flipping pages. An incredible list of names appeared before my eyes. "This is the roll-call for spiritual warriors," I said. "I feel like I'm reading the invitation list for a King's coronation. This is amazing."

A host of familiar and unfamiliar names filled the pages, all men, women and children who had signed the register here in Frontier Town. The inspiring list spanned the Old Testament ages and continued from the early Church to the present. From first century believers and apostles to modern day Christians, every name was handwritten. Some signatures were familiar, but many more were people unknown to me; common names such as Mary, Robert, Frederick, Alice and Nancy. Toward the end of the list, near my own name, were some personal acquaintances, men and women I know whose lives have incredibly blessed me.

"I know that every name in this registry is someone very special and loved by God," I said. "He has called each one of us to follow Him."

I closed the registry and carefully placed it on the desk top. As I turned to leave, the words of Hebrews 12:1-2 surged through my spirit.

"Therefore…since we are surrounded by so great a cloud of witnesses, let us lay aside every weight, and the sin which so easily ensnares us, and let us run with endurance the race that is set before us, looking unto Jesus, the author and finisher of our faith, who for the joy that was set before Him endured the cross, despising the shame, and has sat down at the right hand of the throne of God" Hebrews 12:1-2.

WITH ALL MY HEART

I stepped through the door and closed it behind me. The cold night air of Frontier Town blew over my face. Mounting Spirit Wind, I gave him a gentle nudge. He turned and trotted back up the street and into the darkened distance. The lights from the windows of Main Street faded and disappeared, but the stars still continued their celestial symphony, lighting our way.

What will tomorrow bring? I wondered. My finger traced the words printed in raised ink on the small card in my hand. I repeated the words in a soft whisper, *"Searching for a city whose builder and maker is God."*

Spiritual pioneer! I thought. *With all my heart and being I truly am a spiritual pioneer.*

My eyelids blinked with the heaviness of needed rest and finally surrendered to sleep. The faint glimmer of dawn was just breaking far to the east of Frontier Town, but I didn't notice. I rode on, fast asleep atop Spirit Wind.

Chapter Ten

KINGDOM CREATIONS

I wrestled the sleep from my eyes, twisting my clenched fists against them in half-circles like a biker revving his motorcycle. "Where am I?" I mumbled as my surroundings came into focus. My outstretched legs rested on a patch of green grass. Small yellow and blue wildflowers were growing all around me. The spreading leaves of the oak tree I was leaning against provided a canopy of shade. Spirit Wind whinnied to notify me of his presence, and then resumed his contented grazing in the meadow.

"Judging from the heat, it must be late morning already," I said, recalling the all-night ride across the plain. I had no idea how far we had traveled through the darkness or how long I had been asleep. *This is getting to be a habit,* I thought. *God makes good use of your time when you're in Frontier Town.*

HOMEWORK

The sound of splashing water nearby reminded me of the beautiful meadow and waterfall I had visited months ago with Gillar and Mannor.[1] "It must be close by. **That must be why you brought me here, Spirit Wind,**" I said gratefully, stretching with a giant yawn. "**I feel refreshed just being in this place.** This would be a good time to update my field manual."

Removing it from my shepherd's bag along with my pen, I enthusiastically opened the manual to the Table of Contents just to be certain, and then quickly flipped to the last page of the book. "Here it is, just as I suspected!" I said, with an air of cocky self-assurance, as though I were already a seasoned veteran of Frontier Town. "Chapter One is at the end of the field manual, in reverse order, just like Main Street."

THE CONSTRUCTION SITE

An artist's sketch of the construction site appeared at the top of the page. "Chapter One" was written underneath it. The rest of the page was empty. *There's a lot of homework to do here in Frontier Town,* I thought. *I'd better get busy.*

Every one of us is a work in progress.

I chose "A Work in Progress" for the chapter title and then quickly proceeded to fill the page with the lessons I had learned at the construction site.

First I sketched the three surveyor's stakes exactly as they had been positioned on Main Street, going to great lengths to describe each pin and what it symbolized. As I jotted down my thoughts, I felt as though I were reliving my journey into The Hidden Kingdom with Jesus.[2] Then I drew a line to represent the woven white cord that connected the stakes. With no action on my part, I watched in amazement as the red and gold threads miraculously appeared on the cord, circumnavigating and embellishing its entire length.

On the opposite page I wrote the Scripture references that I had discovered in the stack of lumber, listing them in their proper order. Finally, I described the blinding light generated by the fourth surveyor's pin and made a decent attempt at drawing a picture of it suspended over the site.

I closed chapter one with a succinct, erudite synopsis. "Things aren't what they seem to be in Frontier Town! I must be careful to see with spiritual eyes. This is a supernatural place; it can only be understood in the spirit. This construction site represents my life! There are a multitude of construction sites here just like mine. No doubt God is equipping all of His servants to fulfill their destinies. Every one of us is *a work in progress.*"

ABRAHAM'S PLACE

Chapter Two followed on the next page. A neat sketch of the log cabin appeared at the top. I wrote the words "ABRAHAM'S PLACE" under it for a title. I felt impressed to use upper case letters to acknowledge its importance.

How appropriate, I thought. *Abraham's Place should be at the beginning of Main Street in Frontier Town. He truly is the father of every spiritual pioneer. His faith is the hallmark of every one of God's warriors. No wonder Jesus insisted that we start at this end of the street.*

DISCOVERING YOUR DESTINY

I jotted a subhead beneath the chapter title: "Discovering Your Destiny." Following it, I listed the lessons I had learned at Abraham's Place.

1. No one can proceed past Abraham's Place without permission from God and proper credentials. There are some who try, but fail. Like Lot, they are impostors.[3]

2. No one is worthy or able in and of themselves. Only Jesus makes us worthy! He *is* our credentials! He is our reference. The Holy Spirit is our Guide.

3. God requires all of His spiritual pioneers to make a radical, revolutionary pledge to leave the comfort and convenience of the familiar and accepted in order to fulfill His will. You must be willing to abandon the past and forge ahead by faith. This may mean departing from the spiritual, cultural and geographic landscape that you are used to. You must be willing to give up family and relatives if need be. It's not what others think that should determine your destiny.

4. You must surrender your need to know the end from the beginning. In order to be a spiritual pioneer you must walk by faith.

5. Don't stop short of the full purpose of God. Don't settle down on the journey. Choose to be a pioneer, not a settler. Like Abraham, keep on keeping on. Remember the vow, "Going on still!"

6. Nothing less than a hundred percent, completely sold out, totally abandoned, radical pursuit of God's purpose will do. If you're going to be an end-time warrior, total commitment is an absolute necessity!

7. Follow God's leading explicitly.

8. Let God choose your traveling companions.

At the bottom of the page I wrote a final summary. **"In order to fulfill your destiny you must Get Up, Give Up, Get Out, Go and Don't Stop!"**

REMEMBER YOUR PLACE

I pulled my business card from the pouch and pushed it snugly into the spine of the field manual to mark the page. *It'll be safe here at Abraham's Place,* I thought, smiling.

Flipping back to the Table of Contents, I tilted my pen to fill in the chapter titles. To my amazement the words were already written there. "They must have been recorded here supernaturally as I wrote them on the title page of each chapter. This is some writing instrument!" I exclaimed, staring with admiration at the gold pen in my hand with the appreciation of an experienced scribe.

TIME TO GO

I closed the book, fastened the lantern buckle securely to the silver sword clasp and placed it back in my shepherd's pouch. I glanced around at the refreshing meadow with heartfelt appreciation. *How good God is,* I thought. *Even in the midst of the journey, He provides a place for us to rest and reflect.*

Spirit Wind scampered once around the meadow to loosen his muscles, then trotted straight up to me and eagerly nudged my hand with his muzzle. "All right," I said, stroking the satiny fur of his winter coat. "Let's go!"

THE POTTER'S WORKSHOP

The noonday sun blazed overhead as Spirit Wind hit his stride, kicking up a cloud of dust on the trail. He moved easily over the terrain and it wasn't long before Frontier Town came into view. With single-minded intuition, Spirit Wind sprinted straight up the road and came to a sudden stop directly in front of the Potter's Shop on Main Street.

The potter gave a quick, beckoning wave from inside, just beyond the open door, then deftly returned his hand to the lump of clay he was shaping on the slowly turning wheel. Searing, white-hot fire flashed and sputtered in the bowels of the handmade brick kiln behind him.

"Help me to see with spiritual eyes, Lord," I prayed as I dismounted Spirit Wind and gave him a loving pat. I loosened the saddle slightly, then turned and walked toward the shed.

Who is this man? I asked myself. *That friendly wave sure gives me the impression he's been expecting me; and his dark blue shirt, I recognize it. He's one of the men I saw at Abraham's Place last night.*

HOW CAN THIS BE?

"What'cha making there?" I said, trying to sound like a real cowboy as I stepped through the wide open door. The heat hit me like the breath of a blast furnace. The combination of the temperature outside and the heat from the kiln made the shed's interior a sauna in the desert. The open door admitted adequate light, but not a single wisp of cool breeze blew through it.

"You will soon see!" He replied, with a deep Middle Eastern accent that took me aback.

I was so stunned by the dialectic oxymoron that my mind could not connect the dots. Logic failed me. His vernacular was so totally unanticipated I just couldn't understand what was happening. *How can this be? Not here in the American West, and certainly not in Frontier Town,* I thought, wincing from mental frustration.

He spoke again, never shifting his attention from the clay he was manipulating on the pottery wheel. **"Things aren't what they seem to be in Frontier Town, are they?"** His unfaltering words of wisdom sunk into my being like nails in a wooden beam.[4]

"Yes, I'm realizing that more every day," I said, fumbling over my words. I moistened my lips in the superheated air, still trying to process the initial shock of his accent.

EXPLORING THE WORKSHOP

"Now that you're here, feel free to take a look around. There's a lot to see in *my* shop," the potter said, as he applied noticeable pressure to the malleable clay in his hands.

"Don't mind if I do," I said warily, wondering why he had emphasized the word "*my*" and what could possibly make this shop different from others.

Despite the extreme heat that filled the confined workshop, I felt strangely at home. "I guess you get used to this heat after a while?" I said, wiping my brow. In seconds I was captured by the myriad of details and intriguing pottery in the shed. "I love this place!" I shouted from the back corner, hungrily exploring every nook and cranny with delight. "I don't want to miss the smallest detail."

The walls were lined with dusty shelves that held an incredible variety of pottery in various stages of completion. On the floor in one corner, broken pieces and chunks of jars and vessels lay in haphazard, scattered confusion in a two-foot high square wooden bin.

NOTHING IS WASTED

I leaned over the heap of shattered scraps that were apparently destined to be discarded. "Wait a minute," I said, in amazement. "Each piece of broken pottery has been carefully marked. Every one them has a number on it. This isn't a waste bin, as I first thought. Why, it looks more like an archeologist's collection of fractured and broken potsherds. These are priceless artifacts waiting for attention. When carefully sorted and put in order, the vessels can be reconstructed and restored. Who knows what priceless value may be sitting in what I thought was a waste bin?"

I stood gazing at the heap of broken pieces. Their earthen tones formed a beautiful multicolored mosaic as the light from the super-heated kiln flickered across them. An inexplicable compassion began to rise up from deep within me. Every possible shade of clay was represented in this array of potsherds. *It's like looking at mankind,* I reflected, *every race and tribe all made from the dust of the earth, so broken and fragmented, but so precious and priceless.*

A wave of compassion swept over me. Tears rolled down my dry, dusty cheeks. "These broken pieces have been preserved so the potter can refashion them into whole vessels again," I said. "They're not useless, good-for-nothing garbage. No, they're waiting to be restored."

"What kind of pottery shop is this?" I pondered. "Miracles must be performed here. What kind of potter can take something so broken and devastated and make it new again?"

A SURPRISING DISCOVERY

A rectangular wooden crate resting on the floor just a few feet away along the left wall of the workshop demanded my attention. It sat parallel to the wall just beneath the bottom shelf. The box was long, narrow and of considerable depth. The black-ink label on the exterior side of the wooden box read, "Manufactured by Kingdom Creations." I cautiously opened it, thinking it might contain something fragile. I was surprised to find, lying in long bundles of ten or so strands, very high quality lantern wicks designed for use in oil lamps.

Next to the box, in a continuous line extending to the front corner of the building, were earthen jugs with securely sealed lids. They were all filled with virgin olive lamp oil.

Chapter Eleven

THE POTTER'S HANDS

My path of exploration led me back to the open doorway of the workshop. I stood in front of the potter, watching his hands skillfully shape the clay vessel he was turning on the wheel. From time to time he would dip his puckered left hand into the pail of water sitting beside his stool. Lovingly, he applied the moisture to the clay surface. It yielded to his pressure, flexing with renewed pliability. The wet, earthy smell emanating from the moist clay refreshed my senses.

The potter worked with knowledgeable accuracy. He appeared to be shaping the vessel according to some predetermined design. Every now and then he lifted his face from the wheel and looked off into the distance with a prayerful gaze, as though he were inquiring or referring to an unseen design book for details regarding this particular piece of pottery. On occasion, after these prayerful pauses, he would reach down to his right and gather up a glob of freshly-dug clay from a container and gradually begin to work it into the vessel on the wheel.

He proceeded with strength and compassion. He did not hesitate to apply pressure when it was required. His fingers moved with nimble creativity. *With such dexterity, I'm convinced he's able to make each vessel unique from all the others,* I thought, watching in admiration.

INSIDE THE VESSEL

Suddenly, for no apparent reason, the potter's fingers dug into the clay like a surgeon invading human flesh. I stared in disbelief. A violent, aching pain instantly stabbed into my gut. I doubled over and fell to the ground in front of the potter's wheel. My emotions burned inside me like acid poured on my soul. Unseen, pointing fingers invaded my heart, exposing the hidden places of my life. Long suppressed memories buried deep inside my psyche, hidden away from prying eyes and anesthetized by time, spewed forth like raw sewage. My pent-up hurt and shame lay exposed like putrid, open wounds, festering in my consciousness.

THE PAIN OF CHILDHOOD

A particular scene surfaced with all of its excruciating emotional pain. I was just a little boy; kindergarten age, I guess. We didn't have a lot; I suppose you could say that we were poor. I loved my mom and dad. I was a good boy, or so I thought. I just wanted to be accepted. I simply couldn't understand why the other kids made fun of me.

I stood there in my tattered blue jeans and suspenders. My plaid hand-me-down shirt hung over my white knuckles. My hair was cropped around my forehead in a home-fashioned bowl cut with one untamable stalk of it standing up on the crown of my head. The kids called me stupid and different. They scoffed at me and called me names. It hurt so badly! I had no place to hide, no place to run away and escape to. I was helpless, vulnerable and impressionable.

"Oh, God," I cried, looking up in desperation at the potter. "It's hurt all of my life. I thought the pain of rejection would go away, but it hasn't." Tears flowed from my eyes. The scene was so vivid, so painful. **The potter didn't ignore me; he just kept on shaping the vessel on his wheel as though that would somehow ease my suffering.**

IT'S MY FAULT

Another wave of gut-wrenching agony tore through my flesh with crippling intensity. The pain of my father's death flashed into my consciousness like an erupting volcano. I writhed on the dusty floor in front of the potter's wheel in anguish. "Why didn't I do something?" I cried. "I could have prevented it. I should have read the signs that foretold of the impending heart attack."

I relived the horrible scene. I could hear my mother's pleading, desperate screams waking me from a deep sleep at four o'clock on that fateful morning. "Dale, Dale! Get up. I can't wake your father! I can't wake him! Come quick!"

I rushed to his bedside. "There's no pulse, mom," I said, panic stricken. His body was cold, limp and lifeless. I was too late. "He's dead – and it's my fault! I should have known. I should have done something to prevent it. Why didn't I realize that his chest pains were something more serious than indigestion?"

"Why? Why? Why?" I screamed, pleading with the potter to alleviate my torment. The wheel stopped, and the potter bent close to the clay. With studied precision, he pressed his thumb into the yielding surface. When he removed it, only his fingerprint remained. The agonizing pain of blame and guilt in my heart gradually subsided. I gasped for air like a newborn struggling for life. The relief was wonderful, but short-lived. The wheel began to revolve again.

A DROWNING WARRIOR

I watched with foreboding as the potter's hands shifted to the upper body of the twirling vessel. He grasped its neck in a constricting chokehold. Stabbing, thrusting pain seared into my back like knives plunged deep into my lungs. I wasn't merely wounded, I was mortally stricken. With hysterical desperation, I clawed in the dust like a drowning man frantically reaching for help, for some measure of relief from the cutting pain. I was suffocating!

"What is it, God?" I gasped. "I can't breathe! I feel as though there are knives sticking in my back. The life is being sucked out of me."

Suddenly, all my years of pastoring passed before my eyes. The names and faces of individuals who had criticized me and spoken evil of me flashed before me like wanted posters on a post office bulletin board. Their words of sarcasm and condemnation came at me like daggers, ripping my flesh and injecting my heart with poison.[1]

"I'm so wounded, I'm crippled," I gasped, as though the breath were knocked out of me. "O, God, I can't go on like this. I can't function any more with this bitterness inside me. I'm emotionally exhausted."

SPIRIT WIND

The potter spun the wheel with determination, quickly applying water and adding more clay to the vessel. Droplets of water sprayed from the spinning clay and splashed down upon me. "I'm just clay, Lord," I cried. "I'm just clay! I'm so weak," I whispered in surrender.

I watched helplessly as the potter inserted several fingers into the top of the yielding vessel spinning rapidly on the wheel. I felt like I had been sucked into a cyclone of failure. All of the disappointments of my life welled up within me. My insides were being torn out. "I've failed you, Lord! I've let down my friends and co-laborers in ministry. I've not been the father or husband I should have been. I've wasted and squandered my time and talents. I've even broken covenant and wounded those who loved and trusted me."

I sobbed uncontrollably, reliving the horrible pain of my failures and selfish actions until I could cry no more. I lay in a heap on the dusty, dry floor of the potter's shed, totally undone and broken. The potter's wheel turned more slowly above me and then finally eased to a complete stop. **I lay breathless at the potter's feet. The silence was like death.**

INTO THE FURNACE

The crunch of footsteps fractured the stillness as the potter stepped toward the glowing kiln and pumped the bellows. The air wheezed through the leather accordion, bursting over the glowing coals. Within seconds the rushing air restored the kiln to an effective, usable temperature. The superheated fuel crackled with searing intensity.

Carefully lifting the finished vessel from the wheel, the potter placed it on a singed, metal paddle and thrust it into the midst of the furnace. The flames ravenously encircled the vessel, licking at its surface with cauterizing heat. The momentary sizzling sound reminded me of meat being seared on a grill. The potter laid the shovel aside and closed the kiln door.

I lay perfectly still on the floor of the potter's workshop listening to the roasting clay. My strength was gone. All I could do was reflect on my life. The tests and trials of my Christian walk flashed through my mind: the times I wanted to abandon my call because of difficulties, the haunting question of why others seemed to succeed and prosper in ministry when I didn't, the satanic opposition and spiritual warfare that seemed to be endless, even hopeless.

The heat from the furnace wafted over my despicable dryness in shimmering, mirage-like waves. It was surreal. I imagined that I was the vessel thrust into the kiln, tested and purified by fire. I became aware of my blatant pride and lust for success. Physical infirmities and relationship battles flashed before me. For what seemed like an eternity, I relived the struggles and difficulties I had endured to follow Jesus until I finally surrendered to the emotional and spiritual exhaustion.

WHOLENESS AT LAST

When I opened my eyes from the healing sleep, the vessel was cooling on the shelf amidst the other pottery. I had no idea how long it had been in the furnace or how long I had been lying on the floor in front of the potter's wheel.

I struggled to my feet and brushed the dust from my clothes. "I feel different," I said, looking at the potter through the cloud I had created. "Like a new person in fact. Something's transpired inside of me. I've never felt this way before. I…I feel *whole*," I said, stuttering to find just the right word to describe my condition. Freedom resonated inside of me. The bitterness and stress I had lived with for years was completely gone. "This is wonderful!" I exclaimed. "I'm healed on the inside."

The potter immediately stood up and walked with a noticeable limp toward the finished vessel. He lifted the container from its perch and returned to his seat at the turntable. Setting the vessel down directly in front of me on the wheel, He commenced to examine it with honest discrimination. Ultimately satisfied, he lifted it up to turn it in the afternoon sunlight shining through the shed door. He seemed to peer right through it.

Finally, he flicked his finger on the lip of the vessel, listening carefully to the ringing sound resonating from the rim.

A funny, tickling sensation crept across my stomach. For some strange reason, I had the irresistible urge to sing something. A childlike, innocent song bubbled up inside of me like pure, unadulterated water from a hidden spring.

It was a kind of "Abba" song. You know what I mean, a kind of "Daddy, I love you" refrain with no adult inhibitions. The tune was so transparent that it startled me.

"Almost ready, but not quite," the potter said, and placed the vessel back on the shelf.

BLESSED THROUGH BROKENNESS

"Who are you, sir?" I asked, as he returned to his seat and commenced to form a fresh lump of clay.

"Oh, I'm just a servant of the Lord!" he said, humbly. "I work for the Master Potter. My job, like all the other potters who work for the Master, is to shape and form those He sends to me. He uses many hands to do His work, you know."

"But how do you know what to do?" I asked. "There are so many different vessels here; they're all unique."

"I'm careful to follow His instructions," he confidently replied. "Each vessel must be fashioned according to the details in His master design book. I've also learned some things from my own life that help me in my work here at the potter's shed."

"It's obvious to me that you're very experienced. No doubt you've been well-trained and mentored by the Master. What's your name, if you don't mind my asking?" I said, hoping for an approving response.

"My name is Jacob," he answered, with a wide, somewhat mischievous smile that betrayed his nature. "You know me. I'm the one who wrestled with God. That's why I limp. God had to break me in order to bless me." (See Genesis 32:22-32.)

"It wasn't until after that experience that I learned about making pottery. Before that, I was so proud and full of myself. I thought I could connive and maneuver to get anything I wanted. But once I realized I was only flesh and desperately needed God, my whole life changed. **God had to show me that**

there is only one Ruler in the universe, and I'm not Him. God even changed my name. You can call me Israel, if you like. It means *prince.*[2]

"You see, it's not possible to effectively serve the Almighty as an end-time warrior unless you are first broken by God. Once you have been tried in the furnace, then you can be trusted in His service. He's the Master Potter and we are the clay. He will use many people to shape and mold us into vessels of honor fit for His service."[3]

THE FEEL OF FRESH CLAY

Jacob looked at the clump of moist clay on the wheel. "Come and place your hands here," he said, extending a gracious invitation for me to touch the clay.

The cool, moist substance yielded easily under the pressure of my fingers. Jacob slowly spun the wheel. I watched with delight as the pliable clay yielded to my slightest pressure and began to take shape.

"Remember this lesson well," Jacob said. "The Master will entrust you with the lives of others. When they yield to your authority, do not abuse them or treat them wrongly. They are His servants, and you will one day give account to the Master Potter for your work."[4]

You see, it's not possible to effectively serve the Almighty as an end-time warrior unless you are first broken by God.

"Thank you, Jacob, for teaching me so much. I am forever in your debt," I said with heartfelt gratitude, removing my hands from the precious material.

"You're more than welcome," he replied. "We do Kingdom work here!"

"Yes, indeed!" I nodded in agreement, and turned to leave the potter's shed. Suddenly, I realized that I was limping.

I walked toward Spirit Wind, who had been faithfully waiting for me all afternoon. I mounted the majestic steed and then paused to stare into the potter's shop, searching the shelf for a particular vessel.

"It's me, Spirit Wind," I said. "Do you see that vessel sitting on the display shelf just inside the potter's workshop? That's me!"

SPIRIT WIND

TAKE NOTE

The sun was setting as Spirit Wind and I rode out of Frontier Town. I carefully noted in my field manual the lessons I had learned at the Potter's Shop. Between my tears of loving gratitude and smiles of relief, I scribed each line with the supernatural writing instrument.

First I sketched the vessel representing my life and drew a line through it to divide it into two parts: before and after. The before side showed the multitude of stress cracks; the after depicted the restored, seamless surface. I felt whole just looking at the picture. Then I listed a few key principles:

Only the broken qualify.

Look for those who walk with a limp.

Always stay yielded to God.

Handle God's children with loving care.

I finished the list with a single comment: "I am still on the shelf in the Potter's House. He is still working on me. I will always be the clay. He will always be the Potter."

I signed the page, "A fellow pioneer."

Oh yes, I must give this chapter a title, I thought. *"Jacob's Pottery Shop" will serve perfectly.*

I closed the field manual.

"I've just been through inner healing, Spirit Wind," I whispered. "Go easy tonight. I'm tender inside!"

Chapter Twelve

KOINONIA CAFÉ

"I'm hungry! It's been days since I've had a good home-cooked meal," I grumbled, as the gnawing pains rumbled in my stomach. "I can't wait to get to Frontier Town. There's got to be a good place to eat on Main Street."

Spirit Wind sensed my discomfort and pressed ahead with reasonable haste. The bone-chilling breeze on the dark open prairie cut into my flesh and fueled my appetite. I leaned forward, stretching my torso along Spirit Wind's neck to gain some shelter from the wind. The pulsating sound of his hooves invaded the silent, barren landscape like the churning power of a steam locomotive chugging toward its destination, determined to arrive on schedule.

It was still a pre-dawn darkness when we entered Main Street. The inhabitants of Frontier Town were preparing for another day. The brightly lit windows were a welcome sight. Spirit Wind slowed to a stroll and came to a graceful stop in front of the country restaurant.

FOOD AND FELLOWSHIP

"Thank God," I said, with no disrespect. Balancing myself with a firm grip on the saddle horn, I eagerly swept my leg over the glistening white back of my trusted equestrian friend and planted my feet on the hardened clay of Main Street. The tantalizing aroma of freshly brewing coffee filled the atmosphere in front of the café and wafted down the street like an invisible pied piper, beckoning every person in Frontier Town.

SPIRIT WIND

Exuberant voices drifted past the fluttering curtains through the open windows of the café. A host of people had assembled inside for breakfast. "Well, bless my soul," I said, with the delight of a lonesome pioneer who had just discovered company. "This is the most people all gathered in one place that I've ever seen in Frontier Town."

The inviting charm of the restaurant was all the advertisement it needed. *No invitation required,* I thought, stepping up onto the boardwalk. *No one with good sense would pass by this place; there's plenty of refreshment and fellowship to be found here.* My boots made a lively, thumping sound as I hurried across the raised wooden walkway and stepped through the door into the brightly lit café.

What a delightful place, I thought, as the ambiance enveloped me. The café was crowded with pioneers who were seated around circular tables covered with red and white checkered oilcloth. A constant, happy bantering filled the air as groups of three or more people talked and laughed together. Everyone was drinking steaming hot coffee. A steady flow of traffic moved to and from the huge coffee urn in the back left corner of the room.

THE COFFEE URN

I took the most direct route possible to the coffee urn, weaving around the tables and chairs and brushing past those who were seated on the stools along the front counter. Everyone was so friendly. "Mornin'," many said as I walked past. A few quipped, "New here, aren't ya?"

"Yep!" I replied, with a "glad to be here" tone.

Finally arriving at the coffee urn, I took my place behind the three individuals ahead of me, all wanting refills. The line shortened as each person drew a fresh cup of coffee from the silver urn and speedily rejoined friends around the tables. *At last,* I thought, as the person in front of me drew a full cup. *I'm next!*

I stood directly in front of the coffee urn with my mouth watering in anticipation. **To my total dismay, I realized that I had no cup.** My eyes darted to the left and right, desperately searching the cloth-covered table. "Not a single cup to be found," I said in frustration.

WHERE ARE THE CUPS?

"Where are the cups?" I bellowed, frantically searching around the room in embarrassment. The line was forming behind me with impatient customers, all anxious to draw a fresh mug from the steaming urn.

I felt a sudden tap on my shoulder. Someone in the line directly behind me spoke in a genteel, feminine voice. "What's the matter partner, forgot your cup?"

"My cup?" I asked, in a fog of confusion. "I don't have a cup!"

And then it dawned upon me. "Wait a minute. I do have a cup!" I blurted, with sudden realization "Of course I have a cup!"

I reached confidently into my leather shepherd's bag to retrieve my mug from its resting place. Wasting only a moment's hesitation to admire its utilitarian simplicity, I grasped the plain metal handle with the four fingers of my right hand, thrust it under the spigot and opened the lever. The scorching black column of coffee splashed into the one-of-a-kind vessel.

"I remember the day Jesus gave me this cup," I said, out of the corner of my mouth, loud enough so that the person behind me could hear.[1] The conversation in the room instantly ceased. It was as quiet as Easter morning; you could hear an angel whisper. "Oh no, everyone's overheard my comment!" I gasped, with shyness blistering on my face.

I was suddenly the center of attention. Everyone peered at me.

"Hold it up," someone shouted.

"I want to see it, too," another voice cheered from the far side of the room.

Everyone wanted a glimpse of my cup. Some were even leaning over, straining their necks to get a better view. A few companions at a nearby table clanged their mugs together in a gesture of celebration. Many raised their cups toward me in friendly acknowledgement. Their curiosity assuaged, the clientele resumed their fellowship and soon the buzz of conversation returned to a caffeine-induced pitch.

A DIVINE APPOINTMENT

A single chair sat empty at a table near the center of the room. I maneuvered my way toward it, juggling the hot cup through the crowded cafe.

Moving the steaming mug to my left hand, I shook the heat from my fingers "Sorry to intrude. Mind if I join you?" I asked, interrupting their lively conversation. Before they could respond, I set the scorching cup down.

"Please do!" a gentleman replied, hurrying a glance toward his wife sitting close beside him. She nodded in approval and smiled up at me.

A chair bumped across the floor from the other side of the table and a young man in his early twenties, wide-eyed with youthful zeal, jumped to his feet. "Absolutely!" he shouted. **"I've been waiting for you. My name's Timothy."**

Every person drank from a cup that was strikingly different from all the others.

He stretched his hand out enthusiastically. I gripped it tightly and looked into his blue eyes. "Pleased to meet you, Timothy," I said. "Thanks so much." I slid the empty chair out and took a seat.

That sure was an unexpected greeting! I thought. *He's been waiting for me. I don't even know who he is.*

NO TWO ALIKE

I glanced around the table, trying not to appear nosy. I was intrigued by the uniqueness of each person's cup. The variety of shapes and designs was striking. My observation was confirmed as I surveyed the café. Every person drank from a cup that was strikingly different from all the others.

The young man spoke first, "Tell me about your cup," he requested. "It's so beautiful."

That's odd! I thought. *Compared to some of the other vessels here, why would he consider this plain metal cup to be beautiful? He can't possibly know what's engraved on the inside. Only I know firsthand what incredible wealth the outside of this vessel conceals.*

"Well, this cup is no ordinary cup, son. I've carried it a long way and I keep it carefully protected in my shepherd's bag," I said, patting the leather bag at my side.

"Go on," he said sincerely. "Please tell us your story."

EVERYONE HAS A STORY

My three fellow pioneers huddled close to the table, listening intently. I began my story. "This cup was given to me by my closest and dearest Friend. The two of us have a very special place where we always meet; we call it 'The Secret Place.' One day He showed up with this cup. He told me that my Father made it for me. He said that it was a gift for my journey. It seemed rather plain to me at first, and I still have not learned what kind of metal it's made of. He said it was my very own cup and that I must always drink from it. It was designed just for me. There's not a single one like it anywhere."

I lifted the vessel above the table. Their eyes followed its motion. "See how the handle fits my hand perfectly?" I demonstrated. I watched in delight as my newfound friends clasped their own vessels with cherishing fondness. *They must understand!* I thought. *They act like they have firsthand experience of what I'm saying.*

The husband laid his hand upon his wife's. Her eyes sparkled as she looked at him. They gave each other a loving nod of agreement and touched the rims of their cups together.

"Every time I drink from this vessel I am satisfied. No other cup has ever provided such complete appeasement for my longings and desires." I continued. "This cup is like my life; each time I drink from it, I am absolutely fulfilled. I call it my Cup of Destiny."

Simultaneously, my three newfound friends hoisted their mugs and shouted "Amen!" enthusiastically.

"Amen!" I agreed, and drew my cup to my mouth to take a drink of coffee. My eyes searched the incredible interior of the cup. "You should see what's inside," I said. "It never ceases to astound me. The detail is so beautiful. It's like reading my biography engraved around the inside surface."

The gulp of bracing coffee invigorated me. I tipped the cup again to draw a second swig of the hot elixir. Suddenly, my eyes lighted on a newly engraved inscription about halfway down the interior surface. I could hardly believe what I was seeing. It read, "*Koinonia* Café, Frontier Town."

I sputtered a choking gasp of astonishment, spitting my warm coffee into the air. "I'm here right now!" I wheezed.

My friends were on their feet; the man to my right slapped me on the back. "Are you okay?" he shouted, with genuine concern.

"I think so!" I said, still chocking with incredulity. "What's the name of this restaurant?"

"This is the *Koinonia* Café!" he said. "It's the best place in Frontier Town for food and fellowship. We come here all the time. Wouldn't miss it for anything and we're so glad you showed up to join the crowd."

FRESH BREAD

The word *food* instantly reminded me of my hunger. "I know God led me here. I sure am hungry. Can I get a menu?" I pleaded.

Timothy responded, "Sorry, there are no menus here; but don't worry. The cook knows exactly what you need; you'll never go away from here unsatisfied."

The wife laughed reassuringly. "That's for sure," she said, rubbing her stomach.

The distinct aroma of freshly baking bread emanated from the kitchen beyond the counter. An unidentified voice shouted from the back room, "It'll be ready soon." A cry of glad anticipation arose, and everyone in the room seemed to shout at the same time, "We're starvin' out here, bring it on!"

Within minutes the chef appeared from the back room with an enormous single loaf of bread. He set it on the counter and proceeded to break large chunks from the crusty, steaming loaf. **The pieces of hot bread were passed among the patrons. There was enough to satisfy each voracious appetite.**

I held the more than adequate portion of bread in my hand and bowed my head. "Thank You, Jesus, for this bread of life. Feed my body and soul, and nourish me here in this amazing place called Frontier Town. You really do know what I need before I ask. And, Lord," I prayed, sneaking a peek around the room, "thanks for all the pioneers here at the *Koinonia* Café. Bless them, Jesus."

The bread tasted delicious. Each bite had a different flavor to it. *What an incredible baker,* I thought. *Everything I need is contained in this loaf.* It wasn't long until I was full, and I still had some bread left. I quickly realized that I wasn't the only one with leftovers. All around the room, people were breaking pieces from their slice and sharing it with others. They were laughing and crying as they shared together. Some were bowed in prayer and others embraced each other with a holy affection.

TAKE SOME OF MINE

I turned to Timothy and said, "There's much more here than I need, son. Would you like some of mine?"

"Oh yes!" he replied. "I'd be so blessed to receive from what the Lord has given you."

We sat with our arms around each others' shoulders, sharing and praying together for a long time. It seemed like we were the only ones in the room. Our communion was so deep that when we finally raised our heads to look at each other through tear-filled eyes, no further words were necessary. **We knew that we were called to walk in covenant with each other. I had an overwhelming longing for Timothy to be my traveling companion.**

I could read it in his eyes before he expressed his desire. "Can I come with you?" he said.

"Please," I replied. "It would be my joy, Timothy." I raised my cup from the table to propose a toast. Timothy gripped his own cup with gusto. The two unique vessels met. The noise of the impacting metal sounded through the restaurant like a ringing bell.

The colliding cups jolted my memory. A beloved verse from the Scriptures came to mind. *"Two are better than one, because they have a good reward for their labor. For if they fall, one will lift up his companion. But woe to him who is alone when he falls, for he has no one to help him up. Again, if two lie down together, they will keep warm; but how can one be warm alone? Though one may be overpowered by another, two can withstand him. And a threefold cord is not quickly broken"* (Ecclesiastes 4: 9-12).

I desperately need this young man, I realized with intense longing, *and he needs me.*

"Two by two," I said to Timothy, reflecting on how Jesus called the twelve to Himself, and then sent them out two by two.[2]

I was ecstatic. *This must be how Paul felt,* I thought, *when he met his own Timothy in Derbe while traveling through Celicia. The Scriptures simply say, "Paul wanted him to go on with him." Now I understand how much was left unsaid by this account of the event.*[3] *When two spiritual pioneers meet and God sovereignly knits their hearts together in a covenant bond, destiny is fulfilled and a friendship formed that even hell itself cannot sever. This is a "closer than brothers," Jonathan and David, pact.*

An overwhelming love settled into my heart for this young man. "A traveling companion," I prayed. "Thank You, Father."

COME BACK SOON

Koinonia Café was quickly emptying as its patrons disappeared through the front door and headed down Main Street for various locations in Frontier Town.

"Well, it's time for me to be movin' on," I said, standing to my feet. I drained the last few drops from my cup, wiped the inside and placed it back in my leather bag.

"Thank you for befriending me!" I said to the gracious couple at the table. They both looked up with sincere smiles. "You're so welcome. Please come back soon!" she said.

He stood to shake my hand. "Yes, come back soon. You're always welcome here. The bread's always fresh and the coffee's the best. But you know, the greatest thing about coming here is the wonderful fellowship and the people you get to know."

"I'll be back often; you can count on it," I replied.

By now, Timothy was standing at my side. "Let's go," he said. "I can't wait to see what's ahead."

We walked side by side to the door, shouting good-byes to our fellow pioneers. When I reached out to open it, I noticed, printed in small letters on the top panel, the words: **"Ya'll come back soon for more encouragement."**

"Let me see," I said, straining to focus my thoughts. "I think I remember something from the Scripture that fits here."

Before I could speak, Timothy recited the text. *"And let us consider one another in order to stir up love and good works, not forsaking the assembling of ourselves together, as is the manner of some, but exhorting one another, and so much the more as you see the Day approaching"* (Hebrews 10: 24-25) .

And let us consider one another in order to stir up love and good works....

WE JOURNEY ON TOGETHER

We stepped through the door into the brilliant sunshine. The fresh, light- blue paint on the exterior walls of the café made the wooden sidewalk appear to be tinted.

"Well, Tim," I said, nudging my companion, "have you been here in Frontier Town long?"

"Not too long," he replied, "but I've learned an awful lot in that short span of time."

"Let me show you something," I said, excitedly reaching into my bag to retrieve my field manual. To my surprise, Tim produced his own from a similar leather pouch fastened to his belt.

We sat together on the edge of the raised wooden sidewalk with our feet dangling over the side, studiously writing in our field manuals.

Underneath the sketch of the country restaurant, I entered a title for this chapter, "Koinonia Café." Then I listed the lessons I had learned. When I finished writing, there were still a significant number of blank pages remaining in the chapter.

That makes sense, I thought. *I'll need them for future entries every time I visit the restaurant. This is going to be one of my favorite places. I can't wait to learn the exciting truths and meet the wonderful people I'm going to encounter here.*

I summarized my entry with a few words: "great coffee, wonderful people, very caring and friendly, the best bread in the world. And best of all, I met Timothy here!"

I closed my field manual just as Timothy was finishing his. Peeking over his shoulder at the last entry, I saw in large letters at the bottom of the page, "Thank You, Jesus. I met Dale today." It was smudged with his tears. He quickly closed his book and looked at me sheepishly.

"Thank You for the cup of my life, Lord." I prayed. I knew without needing to look that Timothy's name had been engraved on its interior; it had to be, because it was written upon my heart.

I glanced impulsively over at Spirit Wind, wondering what lay ahead for Timothy and I as traveling companions and fellow pioneers in Frontier Town. His stalwart frame showed no signs of movement. At least for now, he seemed content to stand at ease in front of the café.

"Let's just sit here for a while, Timothy," I said. "No sense in hurrying. I'm sure the Lord has our itinerary planned. Whatever it is," I reasoned, "we are men of like passion, totally committed to pursue God's purposes and possess the future in Jesus' name."

Chapter Thirteen

UNIVERSE-CITY

The sudden, unexpected peal of a thunderous bell startled us both. The clamorous sound came from close by to our left. It clanged over our heads and tolled its message down Main Street with audacious self-assurance. Before the sound could dissipate, the clapper struck again with full force. I felt my chest vibrate in response to the powerful oscillations. The tone was deep and sustained. A third peal struck with demanding intent.

Timothy and I jumped to our feet in response to the invitation and headed down Main Street in the direction of the beckoning sound. **"Hurry, Tim," I shouted, "we don't want to be late!"**

We rushed past the partially painted, two-story clapboard building. Just as we stepped past the corner, the bell struck from the tower of the one-room schoolhouse for the fourth and final time. The front door stood wide open, inviting us to enter. Timothy spoke anxiously. "I wonder if class has started?"

Neither of us hesitated. We stepped down from the wooden decking onto the only lawn in Frontier Town. The magnificent carpet of lush, green grass made me curl my toes in my boots as though I could feel it through the leather soles; it was that innate desire to connect with the soil that all men share in common. The scintillating, sweet smell of freshly cut lawn hung in the air around the glossy- white schoolhouse like spring perfume. A single bee buzzed by me with a steady drone. Timothy watched it dart off toward the back of the building.

103

THE SCHOOL HOUSE

"Let's go in, Timothy," I said reassuringly. "I believe we have been summoned here by the Lord."

A multitude of questions raced through my mind. *A one-room school house! Surely there are many grade levels here, but how can they all be taught in one room? And how many students have already entered? Maybe it's full by now; and what about textbooks?*

I patted my shepherd's bag to confirm the presence of my *Field Manual for Spiritual Pioneers* and my pen. I breathed a sigh of relief. *I've got my own book,* I thought. *I can take notes if I need to.*

We rushed forward and climbed the steps to the open schoolhouse door enthusiastically. "Wait a second!" I shouted at the last moment, suddenly recalling my previous experiences on Main Street. I reached over and grasped Timothy's arm, pulling him to an abrupt halt.

Looking sternly at my spiritual apprentice, I spoke with justifiable caution. "Timothy," I said, "I want to alert you to a very important discovery I've made about this place. You must always keep in mind that things aren't what they seem to be here in Frontier Town. You must anticipate the unexpected. Look beyond the surface of things and see with your heart. Open the eyes of your spirit and listen with spiritual ears. I have the distinct sense that this schoolhouse is unlike any other we have ever seen or experienced!"

I turned to face the entrance to the schoolhouse. Apprehension swept over me. My stomach fluttered like that of a high diver perched upon the topmost level of the platform, looking anxiously down at the surface of the pool far below. My stomach muscles tightened. I mustered the courage to take the plunge. I shouted to Timothy, as though the wind were already whistling past us in mid-air. At the top of my voice I screamed, "Jump!" Together we catapulted through the door of what we thought was a one-room schoolhouse.

CLASS BEGINS

"There's no floor!" I gasped, but it was too late. I was falling, spinning, tumbling into another dimension of existence. Timothy was gone, the schoolhouse was gone and Frontier Town was gone. When the motion finally ceased,

I was suspended somewhere in the darkness of outer space looking down at planet earth. An empty black void surrounded me like an icy shroud, enveloping everything in immeasurable, never-ending mystery.

The view from my assigned seat in God's celestial classroom was breathtaking. Time moved at an accelerated pace. The earth revolved beneath me at hyper-speed. Oceans looked like gigantic reservoirs of surging power. Continents passed by in rapid succession, unfolding in one continuous motion like the pages of a colossal, encyclopedic textbook.

Every revolution of the spinning planet read like a chapter in the uninterrupted chronicle of divine and human history. I stared transfixed, in awe at this incredible saga of life. Each scene flashed by like the successive frames of a movie, speeding rapidly across the focused lens of God's perspective.

TEXTBOOK EARTH

The dawn of creation burst upon the stage of time with the speed of light. The stars twinkled all around me in response to the scene. A beautiful garden passed by below and a flaming sword suddenly appeared at its entrance. Then, in a single revolution, the earth was entirely painted in deep blue as water covered the entire planet in a massive deluge.

As each revolution of the earth passed before me, I could see cataclysmic events transpire. Times of peace and times of war, drought, famine and pestilence were all recorded on its surface. At one point, the earth stopped rotating momentarily and then resumed its ceaseless progression.[1]

Dawn, day, dusk and darkness; spring, summer, fall and winter; one seamless drama, ages long, millennia wide, played out on the terrestrial stage beneath me. Blood, fire and vapor of smoke from a million tragedies cried out from the ground and ferociously licked their way, with vengeance and horror, into the atmosphere above the spinning world.

THE HINGE OF HISTORY

And then, it appeared out of nowhere. A single star coursed through the heavens and cast a prophetic glow over the ancient landscape. The sound of singing angels pierced the heavens with hope. But, just as suddenly, the world turned a tragic red. The angelic song was drowned by the dying cries of countless infants.[2] And still the earth continued spinning, like a time clock ticking mercilessly toward the end of an exam.

All of history was instantly, forever divided by this single, earth encompassing event.

Suddenly, creation stood on tiptoe. I grabbed my ears, groping to determine if I were deaf. The extreme silence exceeded the noiselessness of outer space. Heaven was hushed, breathless with anticipation. Something was happening below on the earth that punctuated all of time and eternity.

With a single stroke of His pen, God drew a sovereign line of demarcation in the journal of Divine and human encounter. A flash of intense lightning bolted from the heavens and struck a town near the eastern shore of the Mediterranean Sea.

"Jerusalem!" I shouted. "The crucifixion of Jesus!" I cried. "The pain is unbearable." I watched Him suffer with tormenting anguish and wept with the universe. **The mournful wail of intense agony pierced the halls of heaven, affirming the ultimate sacrifice.**

A waiting silence fell over the spinning planet beneath me. Three revolutions later the sky exploded with joy as the sun burst onto the land of Israel. A shout of victory rose from the earth, "He is risen from the dead! The Son of God has overcome sin and death. Creation has been redeemed. Jesus is alive!" All of history was instantly, forever divided by this single, earth encompassing event.

THE FINAL CHAPTER

I watched in holy fear and dread. The earth continued revolving with relentless intent, spinning toward the final, cataclysmic completion of its chronicles. Times and seasons came and went, each revolution bringing us inexorably closer to the culmination of history and the end of time. A thousand years seemed like a single day. (See Second Peter 3:8.) Days sped past like seconds as the hands of the planetary timepiece sped toward midnight on the last day of God's calendar. Beyond midnight a timeless, unknown, inexplicable eternity waited.

THE CHRONICLES OF CREATION

"This is incredible," I said. "Talk about virtual reality; this is some school-house. I'm a student in the classroom of the universe. My seat is suspended in the heavens, God is the Professor, and the history of the entire world, from the creation to the present moment, is the subject.

"Never, in all of my twenty years of education, have I seen such a panorama of truth. I've majored in history in college and sat in the classrooms and lecture halls of the experts. I've read countless history books written by the most knowledgeable professors in the world. But this far surpasses anything I've learned at their feet.

"If you really want to understand the significance of history and comprehend the meaning of the ages, you must be taught by the One who created time and made the world and all who dwell in it," I concluded. "This is not the history of man, it's the chronicle of creation, a God-penned account of life on planet earth written in the universe."

How foolish it is for men to take God out of the equation and out of the classroom, I thought. *In order to understand the text, you must know the author!*

PASSION FOR THE SUBJECT

The world revolved below me in all of its grandeur and fragility. Intense love rose up within me like water filling a reservoir. I wanted to reach out and wrap my arms around it and hold it in a global embrace. Such a flood of compassion and longing overwhelmed me that it could only be satisfied by taking every human being in the entire world and gathering them in my arms.

"It's the love of the Father," I whispered.

Like the force of all the water contained in the Hoover Dam being channeled through a single pipeline, the emotional pressure was more than I could contain. "Jesus," I cried, "we need more channels to release Your love on the earth. Lord of the harvest, please send more laborers into the world; the fields are so ripe."

"I am, My son." His response came with such promise. "I am! The harvest will be gathered, as I promised, and then the end will come."

THE BIG PICTURE

The exploding charge of rushing air launched me like a human cannonball and sent me catapulting through space. The earth rapidly diminished in size and disappeared. The thud of leather striking wood heralded my landing on the stoop in front of the schoolhouse door. I felt like an astronaut after reentry, dazed and grateful that I had survived.

I shook myself to be sure all of my parts were intact and brushed the wrinkles from my shirt sleeves and trousers. "Some class session!" I declared, with the satisfaction of someone whose questions had been answered and the chronology of the events put in proper order. "Now that's what I call a real history lesson. That was more than an overview – that's the really big picture!"

Timothy was nowhere in sight. *He must still be in school. No doubt that's a good thing,* I thought. *Isn't that what the Apostle Paul encouraged Timothy to do years ago? "Study to show thyself approved unto God, a workman that needeth not to be ashamed, rightly dividing the word of truth"* (Second Timothy 2:15, KJV).

THE MESSAGE OF THE SCHOOL BELL

A flash of light from the silver bell suspended in the belfry above me grazed across my eyes. I looked up in curiosity. "Yes!" I said excitedly. "I can read it now that I'm closer." A fitting inscription was stamped into the bell's silver surface. *"Not with words of man's wisdom."*[3]

Solomon's words reinforced the lesson with convincing accuracy, like arrows aimed through time, striking the bull's-eye. *"Wisdom is the principle thing; therefore get wisdom, and in all your getting, get understanding.*[4] *How much better to get wisdom than gold! And to get understanding is to be chosen rather than silver.*[5] *He who gets wisdom loves his own soul; he who keeps understanding will find good."*[6]

"Solomon really was a smart man, you know!" I shouted to some imaginary pupils in the empty schoolyard. "Take his advice! The universe is your classroom, one large room, big enough for every student. The world is the textbook. The Holy Spirit is your Teacher. God's Word is your study guide. Oh, and never forget the most important fact: **Jesus is the standard by which all of time and humanity is measured and understood. Without Him, there is no wisdom!** Remember this well. It will most certainly be on the final exam!"

CHRIST, THE WISDOM OF GOD

"For it is written, 'I will destroy the wisdom of the wise, and bring to nothing the understanding of the prudent.' Where is the wise? Where is the scribe? Where is the disputer of this age? Has not God made foolish the wisdom of this world? For since, in the wisdom of God, the world through wisdom did not know God, it pleased God through the foolishness of the message preached to save those who believe. For Jews request a sign, and Greeks seek after wisdom; but we preach Christ crucified, to the Jews a stumbling block and to the Greeks foolishness, but to those who are called, both Jews and Greeks, Christ the power of God and the wisdom of God. Because the foolishness of God is wiser than men, and the weakness of God is stronger than men" (First Corinthians 1: 19-25).

"What could be more profound?" I uttered. "Without Jesus, there is no meaning to anything. The pursuit of knowledge without Him is a wearisome journey of partial truths that leads down a trail of desperation and hopelessness to an eternal abyss of deception. Solomon said it well. *"Of making many books there is no end, and much study is wearisome to the flesh"* (Ecclesiastes 12:12).

PRAYER IN SCHOOL

I bowed my head. "Father, Your Word says that if we lack wisdom we should ask You for it. You promise that You will not scold us or be angry because we asked. So, I'm asking You today to grant me wisdom for the way that lies ahead. I'm asking in faith, Father. I have no doubt that You are willing and able to guide me.[7]

"Jesus, reveal Yourself to me. Give me boldness to tell the world that You are the exclamation point of history and eternity. You are the source of life, the divine center of all wisdom and understanding. The fullness of the Godhead resides in Your flesh. You are the ruler over all principalities and powers. Only in You are we made complete.[8]

"I ask this for my fellow spiritual pioneers also, Jesus. I know there are great challenges and opportunities ahead. The opposition is great. We desperately need wisdom, and above all we need Your presence. Walk beside us.

Grant us intimacy and communion with You on the journey. Without Your presence and power, we will not make it to the end. I ask all of this in Your name, Jesus."

TAKING GOOD NOTES

A confidence like that of Enoch marked my stride as I descended the steps and retraced my path through the thick grass toward the sidewalk on Main Street. I had the profound sense that Jesus was walking beside me.

I sat near Spirit Wind on the boardwalk for a long time recording the lessons I'd learned in school. I concluded my notes with an urgent request. "Lord, grant that every spiritual pioneer and end-time warrior would desire the wisdom and knowledge that can only be attained in Your classroom."

The hours seemed like minutes. When I finally looked up from my field manual, Timothy was still nowhere in sight.

What should I title this chapter? I pondered, returning to my text. *What words can adequately capture the reality of what I've just experienced? This is no ordinary, small-town country school.*

In a sudden burst of inspiration, I shouted with delight, "I've got it! This is *Universe-City* in Frontier Town! That's the perfect title." I scribed the words at the head of the page, closed my field manual, fastened the strap carefully and placed my book and pen in my bag.

SELAH!

I mounted Spirit Wind and made a sucking sound in my right cheek. "Chi, chi; let's go, Spirit Wind! Timothy will be along in his own time."

We sauntered down Main Street at an agile trot. "Go where you please, Spirit Wind," I said. "I've got an awful lot to chew on today."

I had complete trust in his ability to follow God's leading.

Chapter Fourteen

THE BUNKHOUSE

Timothy poked my shoulder repeatedly. "Wake up, wake up!" he shouted in frustration.

"All right!" I mumbled, and proceeded to roll over and cover my head with the pillow.

He poked his fingers into my ribs with persistent determination.

"Okay, I give up," I conceded. I shook the fog from my mind and lifted my head to look around. To my surprise, my surroundings were completely unfamiliar.

"Have I been here all night?" I asked, searching through blurred eyes for clues to my whereabouts. My shepherd's bag and sword were lying on the floor next to me. My field manual was lying on the night stand at the head of my narrow, but comfortable, single bed. *This doesn't help me much*, I thought, very perplexed.

I gazed around the room at the Spartan furnishings. A red kerosene lantern stood on a rectangular table in the center of the room. The table had several thick layers of antique blue paint on it, and the large chips in the finish told me it was well used. Two identical drawers were conveniently located underneath the top of the table in descending order. The drawer handles were especially telling. Made of lead-colored pewter, the circular knobs were designed to look like coiled rope.

WHERE HAVE YOU BEEN?

Timothy interrupted my investigation. "I thought you would never get here!" he said, apprehension still quivering in his voice. "When I left Universe-City yesterday afternoon you were nowhere to be seen, so I just came back here. I waited and waited until finally I heard Spirit Wind's hoof beats approaching outside. You were sound asleep when you arrived, so I carried you in and put you into bed."

I threw the brown woolen Indian blanket and white sheet back with my right hand and swung my legs over the side of the bed. My bare feet hit the smooth wood floorboards with a thump. Shivering in the coolness, I reached down with a groan of morning stiffness to reclaim my socks and boots from the foot of the bed where Timothy had thoughtfully placed them the night before.

SIMPLE COMFORT

With my eyes now fully open, I examined my surroundings from the back of the room with careful consideration. A second bed, already made, was positioned parallel to mine against the opposite wall. An identical night stand stood next to it. An oval carpet, made from multicolored cotton scraps and coiled into a continuous ropelike swirl, lay on the floor between the beds. *Too small*, I thought, wiggling my toes inside my cold boots to increase the circulation.

At the foot of each bed were matching oak desks, small but adequate, and wooden captain's chairs made of oak boards and spindles. Each desktop contained an oil lamp, inkwell and quill pen. The stem of each pen glistened with a shiny, polished black lacquer.

Clothes trees, made from square posts, flanked the windows like sentries in both front corners of the room. Pewter hooks were fastened around their tops to provide for hanging coats or clothing.

YOU MISSED BREAKFAST

Timothy lifted a steaming hot cup of coffee from the nightstand on the opposite side of the room and handed it to me. "Hope you don't mind," he said. "I wanted to let you sleep in, so I filled your cup at the *Koinonia* Café a little while ago. Everyone asked where you were. They really missed you this morning. Here! Enjoy!"

"Mind? You must be kidding, Timothy." I said, gratefully accepting the cup of hot liquid. "Thanks for taking care of me. I don't function well without my morning brew." ***How good it is to have a traveling companion,*** **I thought.**

"Where are we?" I asked, after several gulps of warm coffee.

"Don't you know?" he said quizzically. "You've passed this place every day that you've been here in Frontier Town."

I screwed my face up in a frown, making a conscious effort to recall this place in my memory.

"Sorry, Tim," I said, "I don't remember."

"This is the Bunkhouse!" he replied. "It's the building at the end of Main Street, remember? It's the first one you passed on your initial visit to Frontier Town with Jesus, Gillar, Mannor and Malchior. I've been staying here since I arrived a few days before you."

BUNKHOUSE CHATTER

I stood to my feet and clomped to the front of the room. Peering out the window, I could see pioneers moving about Main Street, busily occupied with their training assignments. *We should probably be doing the same thing*, I realized, but kept my thoughts to myself.

Turning back toward Timothy, I walked to the desk on my side of the room and stroked my fingers across the top surface, savoring the texture of the wood grain now worn smooth by years of use. "Very nice," I commented. "It reminds me of the lid on my desk in grade school. I can still recall every gouge, carving and nick in its sullied surface. I sat at the same desk for years, Tim. It became like a familiar map to me."

I slid the chair away from the desk and took a seat, propping my feet on the desktop. Timothy assumed a similar posture at his desk. We sat chatting for a long time about our journeys and experiences as spiritual pioneers. He asked a lot of questions with genuine interest, mostly about my life and the lessons I've learned along the way. He had such a teachable spirit.

I felt such gratitude for this young pioneer. I found myself relating to Timothy as if he were my own son. Our fellowship was rich and sweet. We talked long after my cup was empty. But inevitably I felt a familiar stirring in my spirit. I realized that the Lord was summoning us. I abruptly rose from my chair. "Come on," I said. "We have an appointment with destiny. We don't want to keep the Lord waiting. He doesn't take too kindly to tardiness."

Thank God for the new breed of spiritual-warrior, I thought, turning to gather my gear. *I hope they're all as teachable as Tim.*

THE ESSENTIALS

I placed my cup on the night stand and bent to pick up my shepherd's bag. Securely fastening the leather satchel around my waist, I spoke my thoughts. "Let's see; do I need to carry everything with me now that I have a place to stay here in Frontier Town?" Reaching into my bag, I removed my eye salve and the parchment letter and put them in the top drawer of the night table, making sure that the drawer was fully shut. "Don't think I'll need these today," I reassured myself.

"But I mustn't forget my field manual," I said, lifting it from the top of the night stand where I had placed it during our conversation. My personal business card protruded above the pages, still securely in place exactly where I put it after Abraham gave it to me. Drawing the cord tightly around the top of my shepherd's bag, I turned to go.

ALWAYS BE PREPARED

When I stepped past my bunk, my right foot struck the overlooked metal object lying on the floor beside the bed. With a loud, metallic clang, it skidded across the room and struck the front wall beneath the window. A shaft of light from the silver blade flashed across the ceiling, capturing the room with its power. I rushed to lift the object from the floor. "My sword," I said, mortified. "I almost forgot my sword!"

"But wait," I hesitated, "what could I possibly need a sword for, here in Frontier Town? This is the last place where one might need to use a sword."

I was about to turn around and leave it for safe keeping on the bed until I returned, when I was stopped in my tracks. An inner prompting, almost an audible voice, spoke inside me. I knew that it was the Holy Spirit speaking to me. "You will need your sword today! Take your sword!"

The gold handle glistened with kingly radiance. "The sword of the Lord," I said, in hushed words of respect. Running my left hand along the silver shaft, I turned the blade from side to side, examining its flawless surface. "The Spirit and the Word," I reflected. "I remember well the day the Lord gave it to me. It's really His sword, but I'm privileged, like many others, to use it."

I shifted my shepherd's bag further to the right, cinched my leather belt another notch and shoved the point of the blade deep into the custom crafted scabbard until the handle sat securely on its leather top. "It's in easy reach if I should need it," I said. I gazed admiringly at the gold hilt which stood out against the dark brown leather. "I have grown so accustomed to this sword hanging at my side that it seems like it's a part of me now."

Timothy was itching to go. I quickly straightened the covers on my disheveled bed, tucking them tightly at the bottom and sides. With a final sweep, I brushed my hand to remove the wrinkles from the woolen blanket.

"All set!" I said. My sense of satisfaction evoked childhood memories. I chuckled and confessed to Timothy, "I can still hear my mother's voice. She always asked me, 'Did you make your bed, son?' before I left for school."

Chapter Fifteen

OVERCOMING YOUR FEARS

It was high noon when Timothy and I stepped out of the bunkhouse. A crowd of people were milling about Main Street, moving at an unhurried but deliberate pace. The eclectic variety of individuals created a surreal scene. The diverse assortment of races, nations and ages were dressed in the traditional clothing of their own culture. It looked more like the concourse at O'Hare International Airport in Chicago than Main Street in Frontier Town.

They're all spiritual pioneers, I reminded myself. *God has summoned them here for training, just like Timothy and me. How blessed I am to have them as my colleagues in combat. We're all end-time warriors in basic training for the final conflict. The greatest harvest of souls in all of history is waiting for us. We need all the warriors we can get!*

GREETINGS, SPIRIT WIND

Timothy pointed down Main Street toward a high-pitched, whinnying sound. "Look! There's Spirit Wind!" he shouted, with the excitement of a child at an amusement park. Before he had finished speaking, he was already moving in that direction. I had to rush to keep pace with his youthful zeal. We dashed down the boardwalk past the yellow, three-story building and the low, windowless storage shed with its adjoining silo. Our boots clomping along the plank sidewalk sounded like horses galloping over a wooden bridge. We arrived, breathless, in front of Spirit Wind.

SPIRIT WIND

The white stallion pranced back and forth in the dust. Suddenly, he reared up on his hind legs in front of us, threw his head back and, kicking into the air, he thrust his muscular frame around in circles, staking claim to this spot on Main Street. Satisfied that he had communicated his intentions, he lowered his head and pawed in the dust with his hooves.

"I think he's trying to tell us something," I said. "Come here, Spirit Wind. Come on," I called from the boardwalk, but he would not budge from his position. His deep, black eyes were clear and alert. His ears stood upright to capture the slightest sound. He insisted that we go to him.

He lowered his head to receive my outstretched hand. Timothy stroked his soft, sleek neck, and patted his angular, perfectly-shaped forehead with affection. *How incredibly blessed we are to have such a faithful companion and wise guide,* I thought.

TODAY'S ASSIGNMENT

Our friendly greeting graciously acknowledged, Spirit Wind stood to attention and moved his head up and down, motioning toward the building behind us. Satisfied with this final gesture, he contentedly stood at ease, staring up at the front of the building. In my haste to greet him, I hadn't noticed where we were on Main Street, but his deliberate prompting brought me to my senses. He was motioning toward the country store.

"That must be our assignment for today," I stated, unnecessarily. Tim had already gotten the message.

"Hmm, the country store?" I said, looking up at the green-shuttered, white frame building apprehensively. "I wonder what the Lord's going to teach us today. There's got to be some provisions we need inside. Look at the amazing variety of goods on those grocery shelves," I said, pointing through the window.

"Been here before, Tim?" I asked, nervously. "Know who tends this place?"

"Nope," he replied, wiping his wrinkled forehead anxiously with his right hand. "Don't know!"

CONQUER YOUR FEAR

Neither of us moved toward the building. Unanticipated fear swept over me with paralyzing power. I trembled in my boots like a recruit preparing for battle with the dreaded realization that this was the real thing and not just a training exercise. I had an overwhelming urge to escape back to the safety and security of the bunkhouse. *Perhaps I can take an afternoon nap, do some reading or study my field manual,* I thought, searching for a legitimate excuse to accommodate my cowardice.

I struggled to understand my unreasonable reluctance. *Why am I searching for an excuse to avoid this assignment? I have no reason to be afraid of a grocery store. This is stupid! After all, it's just a place to buy provisions. What could possibly be so intimidating?*

AN APOSTOLIC EXAMPLE

"Well," I said, summoning my courage. "There's no alternative! Our path has been determined by the Lord." I wasn't looking for affirmation from Timothy or even encouragement for that matter. I was intentionally making a declaration of faith.

"I am committed to obey God's will!" I vowed. Renewed resolve rose up within me simply by speaking the words.[1] "No matter what the cost, I will follow Jesus. We are end-time warriors, Tim. We must not stop short of fulfilling God's entire plan even if the way is difficult.[2] Remember the Apostle Paul's response to Agabus?" I asked. "We must follow his example."

The scene flashed before me with encouraging appropriateness. Paul was spending time in Caesarea at the home of his friend, Phillip.

"… a certain prophet named Agabus came down from Judea. When he had come to us, he took Paul's belt, bound his own hands and feet, and said 'Thus says the Holy Spirit, 'So shall the Jews at Jerusalem bind the man who owns this belt, and deliver him into the hands of the Gentiles.

Now when we heard these things, both we and those from that place pleaded with him not to go up to Jerusalem. Then Paul answered, "What do you mean by weeping and breaking my heart? For I am ready not only to be bound, but also to die at Jerusalem for the name of the Lord Jesus."

So when he would not be persuaded, we ceased, saying, 'The will of the Lord be done.' And after those days we packed and went up to Jerusalem" (Acts 21: 10-15).

"They packed and went up to Jerusalem! That really nails it, Tim," I said. **"Sometimes you just have to pack up and go!** Paul may have been frightened by the intimidating circumstances, but he didn't even allow a warning from one of God's anointed prophets to deter him. What's so surprising is that his traveling companions loved him more than they loved the will of God. It broke his heart. Their personal feelings were getting in the way of God's plans."

MARTYRDOM

"What is it that makes a person obey God's will even when it means persecution, imprisonment or the ultimate sacrifice, martyrdom?" Timothy asked.

"I'm not sure," I replied. "I think it's love."

"I want to be brave," he said, "but I guess I really won't know what's in my heart until I have to make the choice myself. Even when I have the best of intentions, my flesh is so weak.

"Peter's failure is actually an encouragement to me," he continued. "Peter said, 'Even if I have to die with You, I will not deny You.'³ Look what happened to him. He denied Jesus three times in the same night. Presumption, I suppose," Tim speculated.

"Perhaps," I replied, "but I believe he meant every word he said. It was his wholehearted intention to follow Jesus to the end. Peter may have lost that battle, but by God's grace and the restoring mercy and love of the Savior, he won the war! When Jesus healed Peter's heart, He revealed his destiny.

"Do you remember what Jesus said, Tim? *Do you love me, Peter?'* That was the key. Peter replied, *'Lord you know all things. You know that I love you.'* Jesus said to him, *'Feed My sheep.'*

"But Jesus didn't stop there. Here's the clincher:

'Most assuredly I say to you, when you were younger, you girded yourself and walked where you wished; but when you are old, you will stretch out your hands, and another will gird you and carry you where you do not wish.' This He spoke, signifying by what death he would glorify God.[4] *And when He had spoken this, He said to him, 'Follow Me' "* (John 21: 17-19).

COMMITTED TO THE END

"I think I know my own heart, but so did Peter," Timothy admitted. "I want to follow Jesus with everything in me, just like he did; but I'm just not sure I have what it takes. It's not a lack of faith. It's a realistic admission of my human frailty. I don't know what will manifest in my heart when the test comes."[5]

"I *know* you love Jesus," I said, reassuringly. "You wouldn't be here in Frontier Town if you didn't. He sees what's in your heart. Our weakness is His strength.[6] By His grace we can overcome any obstacle, any fear!" [7]

A sudden rush of Holy Spirit unction swept into my soul. "We're not talking defeat here," I shouted, like a football coach with the score tied and only a few seconds remaining in the game. "We're talking total victory! Let's take the high ground, Tim. We're destined to win!

"Committed to the end!" I shouted in a burst of enthusiasm, raising my right hand for a high five.

Tim's countenance radically changed. The Holy Spirit came upon him. His spirit, soul and body were instantly saturated with the presence of God. He was glowing.

"Committed to the end!" he affirmed. Smacking his hand against mine with all the strength he could muster, a hopeful grin was plastered across his face. The moment was priceless, life-changing, irrevocable!

"Remember what the Word promises, Tim. *"If two of you agree on earth concerning anything that they ask, it will be done for them by My Father in heaven."*[8]

With bold courage and confident faith, I looked at Timothy and said, "Let's go, son! Our divine destiny is waiting."

TO BE CONTINUED

We stepped toward the Country Store, but it faded from view before we could reach it. "No," I gasped, in desperation, as Frontier Town dissolved before my very eyes. The Well of His Presence flashed before me and then it too was gone. "Oh, Lord, not now, not yet," I pleaded, but to no avail. My time in His presence was over.

Disappointment and frustration hit me all at once. "What comes next?" I said in frustration, like someone watching an installment in a television series when the action is cut at the most intense moment of suspense.

"To be continued," I heard the Holy Spirit say.

I closed my journal and reluctantly laid my pen down. "I can't wait to see what happens next, Lord."

Chapter Sixteen

THE GENERAL'S STORE

From the moment the vision of Frontier Town first appeared to me, I had been totally captivated by its intrigue and mystery. Each day flew by, filled with new discoveries and adventure as I sat in God's presence waiting for further revelation. My Secret Place became a habitation for the Holy Spirit. The unfolding saga was so fascinating and delightful that I never wanted it to end. By now, I knew Main Street like the palm of my hand. I just didn't know what existed inside the remaining unexplored buildings.

BACK TO THE WELL

"I'm learning so much about myself and what it means to be a spiritual pioneer, Holy Spirit," I said, as my study door banged shut and I twisted the lock. "I feel like I'm finally growing up spiritually. I can't wait to get back to The Well of Your Presence and Frontier Town. Spirit Wind must be raring to go."

I eagerly opened my journal and bowed my head. "There's so much to learn, Jesus," I prayed. "I dedicate this time entirely to You. No phone, no music, no distractions, Lord, just You and me here in this Secret Place. I want to be with You so much, Lord.

"Clear my mind of ideas that are not from You. Free me from distractions that silence Your voice and hinder our communication. Cleanse my soul the residue of worldly activities and the defilement of fleshly ar nothing impede my ability to hear Your voice, Jesus. May these next few hours be a time of undefiled intimacy and pure revelation.

"I know You have drawn me here to speak to me. I am here on assignment. Give me vision, Lord, and complete the revelation of Frontier Town. Let it be a blessing to Your Church. I come to The Well of Your Presence, Jesus. Thank You, Lord. I know that You have been waiting for me."

IT LOOKS LIKE A COUNTRY STORE

In moments, I was back in Frontier Town standing next to Timothy in front of the country store. The bright sun reflecting off the yellow clay street gave a mustard tint to the showcase windows on each side of the front door. They glistened like giant mirrors, reflecting the images of Frontier Town.

"I can't see inside, Tim," I said, my nerves quivering with heightened attentiveness like popping electrical circuits.

"Neither can I," he snapped back.

The closer we moved toward the country store, the more I realized that it was not what it appeared to be. We cautiously climbed the steps and tiptoed onto the wood plank docking like soldiers entering a minefield.

"All I can remember is that I saw an antique mailbox in the center of the store," I said in hushed tones. "You know, it looked like something you might see in an old frontier post office. There were small compartments, like post office boxes for sorting mail by name. Oh, and the walls were lined with shelves, too, stocked with all sorts of provisions. Well," I whispered, trying to assuage my apprehension, "from what I can recall, it looked like a country store then; but I'm not so sure now."

DID YOU HEAR THAT?

Tim's face turned as white as a ghost and his mouth fell open in disbelief. We looked at each other in shocked dismay, our eyes bulging.

"Did you hear that?" he said.

"We've got to do something!" I replied with alarm.

We both heard the unmistakable, sustained cry coming from inside the store. It wasn't a distress call from someone in danger. It sounded more like someone charging into battle, screaming with incredible fury.

My hand instinctively moved to grasp the hilt of my sword. "Come on, Timothy!" I shouted, my heart pounding like a timpani. I grabbed the door handle and thrust it open forcefully, letting it slam against the outside wall of the Country Store.

We leapt through the entrance like Special Forces charging the enemy, every faculty alert to what we might encounter. We were instantly cloaked in total darkness. **There seemed to be no floor in the country store. It was like parachuting from a plane at night into a moonless, starless blackness.** I reached to see if Tim was by my side. My hand grazed his shoulder and he jumped, startled by my touch. The silence was deafening.

"Shhh," I whispered, but it sounded like I was shouting. "Don't move!"

We stood perfectly still, every muscle taut with postured anticipation. Slowly, our eyes adjusted to the darkness. Strange, unidentifiable shapes began to take form all around us. My mind struggled to make sense of it all. My hand was moist with perspiration as I clutched the handle of my sword, ready to draw it at a moment's notice.

WHAT'S THAT SMELL?

An almost imperceptible wisp of air passed over my face. I strained to identify the smell, sucking the moldy moisture into my nostrils. A damp, musty odor surrounded us like stagnant air that had been trapped in some long forgotten, sealed cavern. *Cavern*, my thoughts shouted at me in sudden revelation.

"We're in a cave of some kind, Tim!" I declared. "From the smell of this stale air, no one's been here for a long time."

We stood in the clammy dampness for several minutes, straining to detect the slightest noise or movement. Finally, Tim spoke. "I think I hear water dripping. I can just barely detect the sound. It could be a spring or a pool of water deep inside the cave."

I turned my head to focus my hearing, and listened with all the acuity I could summon. "I hear it now," I replied. "Barely, but I can hear it."

SPIRITUAL SPELUNKERS

Our pupils were fully dilated now. "No one's here," I said reassuringly, peering through the darkness. "Let's check this place out."

"You go ahead," Tim responded. "I'll guard your back."

We groped through the blackness, exploring the cavern with the careful scrutiny of Sherlock Holmes and his trusted accomplice, Watson. "There must be some clues here that can tell us where the war cry originated from," I said, studying our surroundings. "The Lord has called us here for a very important reason. There's a major lesson to learn."

"I thank You, Lord, that this place is so big," I said, in relief, staring up at the ceiling fifteen feet above me. "At least I don't have to deal with claustrophobia."

The cavern was considerable in size. A detachment of people could easily occupy it without being cramped. My eyes lighted upon a cluster of stones lying in a circle at the center of the cave. **"Look, a fireplace! Someone's been here before us!"** I said, rushing toward the stones. I bent to examine the site. Silver-gray ashes lay in a heap in the center of the fire pit. They were cold and lifeless, no doubt left by someone long since departed.

EVIDENCE

"Come here, quick!" Tim shouted in surprise.

Rushing over to his side, I looked down at the incredible discovery. Lying there among the stones on the cave floor was a shepherd's bag just like the one I was wearing.

"Let's not inflict any more damage than time has already done," I cautioned. I lifted the pouch from its resting place with the astute care of an archeologist removing a priceless artifact from an ancient tell. The once supple leather had hardened and dried to a stiff, cracked, centuries-old brittleness.

"Whoever owned this must have left here in haste," I said. "No self-respecting shepherd would leave his bag lying in a cave."

I opened the rigid bag with miniscule, slight movements, fearful that it might crumble in my trembling hands. I peered into the bag, hoping to find contents that might provide a clue to the identity of its owner.

"Nothing in here but a few pieces of coiled string," I said, disheartened.

Handing the ancient leather pouch to Timothy, I instructed, "Hang on to this, son. It may provide us with some answers later."

CREEPING TOWARD THE SPRING

Satisfied that there was nothing of further importance in the main cavern, we worked our way cautiously through a narrowing passageway that led deeper into the cave in the direction of the spring. At times we had to stoop to our knees to avoid hitting our heads on the ceiling.

"Ouch!" Timothy shouted painfully, as he struck his forehead on a jagged rock jutting into his path.

We squeezed our way through the womb-like passage, scraping and bumping along on our hands and knees. Gradually the dripping sound grew louder, and soon we could hear the steady bubbling of an underground spring. I wrestled my way the last few feet, gripping the stones with my broken fingernails. My sweat lathered my skin like rancid oil. With one final grunt, I pushed my way through the narrow opening and fell exhausted into a dimly lit, very large cavern.

The ceiling towered thirty feet above us. A small entrance near the roof emitted welcome light into the interior of the grotto. The air was much drier and fresher compared to the musty cave we came from. I breathed deeply, sucking the dry oxygen into my lungs.

We both spotted the sparkling pool of water in front of us at the same instant. Not bothering to look around, we dashed forward, knelt down by the edge of the pool, and drew the refreshing water to our mouths in large handfuls, gulping its sweetness and gasping for breath between each chug.

"We've been bent over for hours," Tim said, finally standing to stretch the soreness from his back.

I wiped my mouth with the back of my hand and burped deliciously. "Scuse me," I apologized, "but that's some of the best water I've ever tasted,"

AN ANCIENT ARMORY

My eyes blinked in disbelief at the scene before me. Scattered about, in almost every nook and cranny of the massive grotto, was an incredible cache of primitive weapons. Swords and spears leaned against the rock walls. Knives lay in piles next to a sharpening stone.

"I think we're in an armory," I shouted over to Tim in puzzled astonishment.

My eyes raced around the room, ravenously devouring its antiquated contents. Several large cooking pots sat near a huge fireplace. Pottery vessels of all kinds and shapes were scattered about nearby, all still in useable condition. Animal hides and blankets were rolled and piled in a heap on the floor right where it began to slope upward about forty degrees toward the light flooding into the entrance.

In the recess of the cavern, directly behind us, a small circle was chiseled into the wall at waist height, apparently to provide a target. A pile of walnut-sized stones were gathered in a heap about twenty feet away; several leather slings lay draped over a boulder.

"This is the discovery of a lifetime!" I shouted, with the excitement of an explorer who had just uncovered hidden treasure. "Tim, we're actually standing in a subterranean army encampment."

A host of questions raced through my mind in rapid succession. *Who occupied this cave? Why were these supplies and equipment left here? Were these soldiers mercenaries hiding inside this mountain? If so, what cause were they championing?*

INDIANA JONES

Timothy and I darted to and fro, eagerly examining the habiliments and accoutrements of the unidentified army. Articles of clothing, shields, bows and arrows, swords and knives lay everywhere. It was an incredible treasure trove of artifacts.

"I wonder what it was like to fight an enemy with a bow and arrow?" I asked, aiming the spent bow toward the ceiling and pinching the dry string between my fingers.

"Imagine trying to defeat someone with a sword and shield," Tim said, hiding behind a dented shield and brandishing a rusted weapon in the air.

"I know of one sword that never dulls," I said, glancing at the sword securely fastened to my hip.

We searched the grotto for hours, delighting in the intrigue of each new-found item. A thousand secrets lay scattered on the cave floor. The cavern was a veritable museum of military history, an unwritten journal of daring exploits and courageous combat. Every relic became a clue pointing to an anonymous warrior. *Some of these soldiers undoubtedly fought to the death in hand-to-hand combat,* I pondered, totally engrossed in the imaginary war epic playing out on the screen of my mind.

A SECRET PASSAGEWAY

I resisted the urge to climb to the cave's entrance and retreat back into the sunlight. The definite prompting of the Holy Spirit led me to search further along the walls of the huge cavern. Inching along its circumference, I was carefully examining the contour of the boulders and rocks when, to my surprise, I discovered a small fissure. It was immediately clear to me that no human hand had carved out this fissure from the solid rock. Some incredible force had split the earth open at this particular spot. *An earthquake could conceivably have shaken the ground with such force that it actually split open right here*, I thought.

Squeezing into the narrow crevice, I wedged my way along, taking only small puffs of breath to lessen the size of my chest. Barely able to pull myself along with my fingertips and toes, I rammed my body farther into the passageway, all the while fearful that I might become inextricably lodged between its vice-like walls. At last the fissure widened slightly, and I wriggled wormlike into an open space. My bones clicked and crunched as I stretched the cramps from my compressed flesh.

Several openings just ahead of me led in different directions from the stone chamber. An unlit torch hung from the side of one wall, clearly indicating that at one time this was a frequently used passageway.

This seems to be an intersection of sorts, I reasoned. *I must be in a hallway or corridor of some kind. What clandestine purpose did this place have? And this torch! There must be others like it to light the subterranean passageways ahead.*

I ran my hands over the walls like a plasterer checking his work. "These walls are smooth, especially at my waist. Very puzzling," I said. The walls of the small subterranean room were worn smooth like polished marble. They reminded me of the temple stones I had touched at the Wailing Wall in Jerusalem, their surfaces worn smooth by a million beseeching hands.

I turned back toward the secret passageway with a start. "I'd better get back to Timothy. He doesn't know where I am. He's probably concerned for me by now!"

A MESSAGE CARVED IN STONE

I glanced over my shoulder with regret and reluctantly forced my body back into the narrow fissure. *I don't know why, but I feel an affinity for this place,* I thought. *It seems to beckon me.*

In my mind's eye I could see the faces of men and women moving back and forth through the tunnel, smiling and greeting each other. For just an instant, I thought I heard the faint echo of singing emanating from one of the passageways at the other end of the chamber. "It can't be," I said to myself. "My mind is playing tricks on me. These caves have been empty for centuries."

With one last shove, I slid my hand across the smooth surface of the wall to propel myself further into the narrow crevice. To my amazement, my fingers grazed across an unusual anomaly in the stone. **I froze in place. "It's a message!" I gasped with exploding curiosity.**

My head was wedged into the fissure by now, so I couldn't turn around to look. Like a blind man deciphering brail, I traced the abnormality with my forefinger. The single, curved line abruptly ended at a point, then reversed direction, arching back to intersect the first line.

"It's a fish!" I shouted. "Christians must have carved it here. I've got to tell Tim."

Bursting into the large cavern like a rabbit springing from its hole, I called, "Tim, Christians have been here. I found a carving in the wall. It's a fish!"

"That's incredible!" he shouted back from the far side of the grotto. "What is this place?" he asked.

"I'm not certain, but I have a good idea," I replied. "Let's get out of here!"

We clambered our way up the steep incline to the mouth of the cavern, dislodging the stones and small boulders from their ancient resting places. They tumbled behind us, clattering down to find a new residence on the floor of the cavern. The echoing sound of their descent rattled off into the depths of the amazing, hidden military compound.

What a perfect hiding place, I thought, as we reached the top of the stone pile. "How, in the name of father Abraham, did we get in *here*?" I asked, incredulous.

Chapter Seventeen

THE POST OFFICE

Timothy and I were flabbergasted. The instant we stepped through the cave exit, we found ourselves on the main floor of the country store. Shelves full of jars, tins, boxes and supplies of every sort surrounded us. A rack near the front door displayed brooms and shovels. Sacks of flour and grain were stacked in mounds on the floor. Bolts of poplin and woolen cloth lay on the counter to our right, looking like giant rolls of Christmas wrapping paper. Gallon-sized clear glass jars chock full of multicolored hard candy sat next to a sturdy brass cash register. Just behind the register on the wall, a pendulum clock tick-tocked away, keeping track of the time in Frontier Town.

MAIL CALL

An unanticipated voice greeted us from behind a stack of wooden barrels in the corner. "Better check your mail, boys! It's been here for several days. I wondered when you'd be here to pick it up."

The impressive, seven-foot high bureau-shaped post office stood in front of us in the middle of the country store. Timothy looked at me with an unconvinced expression. "Mail?" he blurted out. "For us?"

We dashed forward like soldiers eager for the latest news from home. Sure enough! There, in clear printing on one of the boxes near the top right side, was a cubicle with my name on it.

Timothy searched frantically for his, but couldn't find it. He moved anxiously to the opposite side of the mail center. I heard papers shuffling and then a sigh of relief. "Here it is!" he said, as he withdrew the items from a compartment on the bottom row. He fell silent, engrossed in reading his mail.

CLUES FROM A PROPHETIC SCRIBE

I plucked the items from my mailbox with fascination. **There were three plain white envelopes, each one postmarked by a single number.** "Hmm; one, two and three," I said, shuffling the envelopes. "These numbers must indicate the order I'm supposed to read them in."

I thrust my finger under the gummed flap, tore the first envelope open and withdrew the two-page letter. "Look at this, would ya!" I whispered, not wanting to disturb Tim on the other side of the mail chest. I tilted the page back and forth, capturing the light from the front window. I watched in fascination. The document contained a watermark that filled most of the page. When I moved it, the transparent image shimmered through the paper like a three-dimensional hologram. The form of a glistening king's crown danced above the paper.

A handwritten reference appeared at the top of the page: First Samuel 23: 14-29. I read the text with the concentration of a detective looking for clues to unravel a mystery.

...David stayed in strongholds in the wilderness, and remained in the mountains in the Wilderness of Ziph. Saul sought him every day, but God did not deliver him into his hand. So David saw that Saul had come out to seek his life. And David was in the wilderness of Ziph in a forest. Then Jonathan, Saul's son, arose and went to David in the woods and strengthened his hand in God. And he said to him, "Do not fear, for the hand of Saul my father shall not find you. You shall be king over Israel, and I shall be next to you. Even my father Saul knows that."

So the two of them made a covenant before the Lord. And David stayed in the woods, and Jonathan went to his own house.

Then the Ziphites came up to Saul at Gibeah, saying, "Is David not hiding with us in strongholds in the woods, in the hill of Hachilah, which is on the south of Jeshimon? Now therefore, O king, come down according to all the desire of your soul to come down, and our part shall be to deliver him into the king's hand."

And Saul said, "Blessed are you of the Lord, for you have compassion on me. Please go and find out for sure, and see the place where his hideout is, and who has seen him there. For I am told he is very crafty.

"See therefore, and take knowledge of all the lurking places where he hides; and come back to me with certainty, and I will go with you. And it shall be, if he is in the land, that I will search for him throughout all the clans of Judah."

So they arose and went to Ziph before Saul. But David and his men were in the Wilderness of Maon, in the plain on the south of Jeshimon. When Saul and his men went to seek him, they told David. Therefore he went down to the rock, and stayed in the Wilderness of Maon. And when Saul heard that, he pursued David in the Wilderness of Maon.

Then Saul went on one side of the mountain, and David and his men on the other side of the mountain. So David made haste to get away from Saul, for Saul and his men were encircling David and his men to take them. But a messenger came to Saul, saying, "Hurry and come, for the Philistines have invaded the land!"

Therefore Saul returned from pursuing David, and went against the Philistines; so they called that place the Rock of Escape. Then David went up from there and dwelt in strongholds at En Gedi."

First Samuel 23:14-29

The letter was signed, "Samuel, the prophetic scribe." I quickly folded the letter, put it back in the envelope and thrust it back into my mailbox.

THE MYSTERY IS SOLVED

"This is remarkable," I said, tearing open the second envelope. My eyes darted across the page. The handwriting perfectly matched the first letter. *Obviously, the same scribe!* I thought. The reference was First Samuel 22:1-2: *"David therefore departed from there and escaped to the cave of Adullam"* (First Samuel 22:1a).

The words struck me with the power of a thousand volts of electricity. **"Aha," I shouted loudly, "The cave of Adullam!"** Timothy's boots banged against the floor as he jumped back in shock on the other side of the chest.

"Sorry, Tim," I called around the mailboxes, "but I can't contain myself. Things are beginning to make sense to me."

I hurriedly read on.

"So when his brothers and all his father's house heard it, they went down there to him. And everyone who was in distress, everyone who was in debt, and everyone who was discontented gathered to him. So he became captain over them. And there were about four hundred men with him" (First Samuel 22:1b-2).

My hands trembled with excitement. "Timothy," I called. "Come here quick! Let me see that shepherd's bag!"

Timothy instantly appeared from behind the mail chest and handed me the antiquated pouch. Searching its surface with microscopic precision, my eyes lighted upon the miniature Hebrew letters hand carved into the hardened leather. My mouth fell open! "David," I gasped.

"Look, here!" I pointed to the small scratches on the brittle surface. "This is *David's* shepherd's bag! We found it on the floor of the cave where he left it. It must have been one of the caves at En Gedi. That's where we must have landed when we catapulted into the door of the country store, Tim.

"And the larger cave," I said, my voice quivering with excitement, "it must be the cave of Adullam. I'm almost positive! Here! Read this letter."

Timothy's eyes were wide with exhilaration as he read the text. "The grotto!" he said, in astonishment. "It could easily accommodate more than four hundred soldiers. I'm sure of it. I didn't tell you, but while you were squeezing through that narrow crevice, I noticed some numbers written repeatedly in the dust on the floor of the cave. Now I know what they mean!"

"Saul has slain his thousands…," Timothy started.

"And David his ten thousands," I replied, before he could finish.[1] "Incredible!" we shouted in unison, staring at each other in shock.

THE THIRD MESSAGE

"This last one must hold the clue to the secret passageway," I said, eagerly ripping open the third envelope. "This is hard to read," I said straining at the document. "Looks like someone scribbled this in free hand; it reminds me of a prescription hastily written by a busy physician. It's Acts 7:54-8:4."

When they heard these things they were cut to the heart, and they gnashed at him with their teeth. But he, being full of the Holy Spirit, gazed into heaven and saw the glory of God, and Jesus standing at the right hand of God, and said, "Look! I see the heavens opened and the Son of Man standing at the right hand of God!"

Then they cried out with a loud voice, stopped their ears, and ran at him with one accord; and they cast him out of the city and stoned him. And the witnesses laid down their clothes at the feet of a young man named Saul. And they stoned Stephen as he was calling on God and saying, "Lord Jesus, receive my spirit."

Then he knelt down and cried out with a loud voice, "Lord, do not charge them with this sin." And when he had said this, he fell asleep.

Now Saul was consenting to his death. At that time a great persecution arose against the church which was at Jerusalem; and they were all scattered throughout the regions of Judea and Samaria, except the apostles.

And devout men carried Stephen to his burial, and made great lamentation over him. As for Saul, he made havoc of the church, entering every house, and dragging off men and women, committing them to prison. Therefore those who were scattered went everywhere preaching the word."

Acts 7:54-8:4

THEY DIED SINGING

The weight of the words slammed into my mind like a freight train. My thoughts raced out of control: *the narrow fissure, the secret passage, the smooth stones in the hidden chamber, the torch on the wall, the fish carved into the stone, the tunnels leading off into the darkness.* It all came together with lightning speed. *Now I understand why I had such an affinity for the place, why I didn't want to leave the secret chamber.*

My lips quivered with passion and grief. "The Catacombs! I was in the Catacombs!" My head fell forward against the mailbox and I began to sob uncontrollably. "My God," I cried. "They died! They were brutalized, beaten and stoned. They were crucified upside down and fed to lions like raw meat. What a price! What a bloodbath. Husbands and wives separated and never reunited. Children crushed with stones, their little bodies broken and bleeding, the very life pummeled from their fragile forms. They hid in the caves beneath the city and carved symbols in the walls.

"Oh God," I groaned, "their singing still echoes through the subterranean passageways of Frontier Town. They died singing! They died singing!"

MEET THE MANAGER

Someone took the letter from my hand and a comforting arm fell across my back. A compassionate voice spoke; his words penetrated deep into my soul. "I know," the man said. "I was there!"

I slowly lifted my head, and through tear-swollen eyes looked into the wizened face of the little man standing next to me. His face bore the wrinkles of a thousand years. A jagged scar, inflicted long ago by an angry enemy, darkened his right cheek. His eyes were old, weak and kind.

"You were there?" I sputtered, wiping my nose on my sleeve.

"Yes! I was there!" he replied, tipping his hat a few inches. "I'm Paul. I'm the manager of the general store here in Frontier Town. In fact, I've personally written mail to every spiritual pioneer who's ever come here."

When he lifted his hand to place the letter back in its slot, a momentary flash of red light reflected off of his ring. "I've seen that ring before, in The Secret Place," I said with deep regard. "You're Paul, the Apostle!"[2] I watched his hand move toward the mailbox and then I scanned across the bureau, reading the names on each compartment. "Paul?" I queried, "This is unlike any country store I have ever seen."

"You're so right," he replied. "This is really not a country store. This is the *General's Store.* Every item needed for spiritual warfare is kept in stock here. You will find everything a spiritual pioneer could ever want. The Lord Jesus, our Commander-in-Chief, has wisely provided everything we need." He spoke with special emphasis when he said *Lord.*

Throughout history, the Lord has summoned His warriors here to receive their training and equipment.

"**Throughout history, the Lord has summoned His warriors here to receive their training and equipment.** They come from a million *Secret Places* throughout the world. They arrive through The Well of His Presence, much like you did, but each one must travel through a different set of circumstances. Some have come from caves in the hills. Others come out of the wilderness, like me, where they have spent years with God. Some are thrust into the store in utter need because of horrible persecution, suffering and crisis. This is where everyone whom God has called to be an end-time warrior must come for provision. This is the General's Store."

MAIL WAITING!

"One thing is of utmost importance," Paul exhorted, shaking his finger in my face with strident boldness. "You must read your mail every day here in

Frontier Town. But unlike other post offices, you're allowed to read everybody else's mail too."

"Really?" I said, to be sure I'd heard him right.

"In fact, I urge you to do just that! Spirit Wind brings the mail into town every morning. If you want to succeed and be victorious as an end-time warrior, you must read the Word God has written to you every day."

Paul turned and walked back to his chores behind the barrels in the corner of the store. "Feel free to look around," he said, "and if you have any questions, just ask me."

WHAT WAS THAT SHOUT?

Timothy and I lingered for hours, perusing the shelves of supplies and reading the mail in other people's boxes, all the while feeling like mischievous kids. It was long after sundown when we finally thanked Paul and said good-bye.

I turned and called back from the doorway. "Paul? What was that shout all about? The one we heard before we came in here this afternoon."

"I didn't hear any shout," Paul said, "but I know one is coming, and it's not too far off.

> '...the Lord Himself will descend from heaven with a shout, with the voice of an archangel, and with the trumpet of God. And the dead in Christ will rise first. Then we who are alive and remain shall be caught up together with them in the clouds to meet the Lord in the air. And thus we shall always be with the Lord'" (First Thessalonians 4:16-18).

SITTING AT OUR DESKS

We closed the door behind us and hurried back to the bunkhouse. Despite the tiredness in my body, I couldn't wait to make some notes in my field manual. We sat at our respective desks like students cramming for an exam. I touched my pen to my temple pensively and then began to record the lessons of the day.

I printed "The General's Store" at the top of the page, tracing over the letters to embolden them. Then, in descending order I listed the following notations:

1. We all arrive here through The Well of His Presence, but the circumstances that propelled us here are unique and costly, often requiring great sacrifice.

2. Wilderness experience is extremely helpful, if not required (i.e., Moses, Joshua, David, Jesus, Paul).

3. The individuals called to lead God's army are men and women who understand and walk in covenant (i.e., Jonathan and David).

4. Men who know failure, distress, debt and discontent make incredible warriors (i.e., the men at Adullam's cave).

5. You don't take authority; it is given to you.

6. Learn to outwit your enemy. Be wise as a serpent and harmless as a dove.

7. Choose your battles; don't let the enemy decide when and where you will engage him.

8. God provides a Rock of Escape. That Rock is Jesus.

9. Persecution brings fruitfulness.

10. Jesus is the Commander-in-Chief.

11. Don't forget to read the mail every day.

12. Keep listening for the final shout.

I tumbled into bed, exhausted. "Good night, Tim," I yawned.

A final fleeting thought passed through my mind. *Didn't I see Paul at Abraham's place when I arrived here? The shape of his hat, that's what it is. He tipped it when he passed me along with the other men, just like he did today at the General's Store.*

The last thing I remember seeing was Tim's fuzzy outline standing over my desk looking at the entries in my field manual and copying what I had written into his own.

SPIRIT WIND

The silence of sleep enfolded me like the woolen blanket Tim lovingly tossed over me to keep me warm through the night. I fell fast asleep on my bed in the bunkhouse on Main Street in Frontier Town...with my sword on!

Chapter Eighteen

END-TIME WARRIORS

The drumming rain splattering on the roof of the bunkhouse sounded like a family of squirrels in the rafters. Thunder rumbled nearby and growled its way across the prairie into Frontier Town. Timothy snored away like a buzz saw on the other side of the room. I peeked from under the blanket. *I wonder what time it is,* I thought.

It was still dark outside the bunkhouse. A warm yellow glow radiated from the lantern on Timothy's desk and sent flickering shadows dancing across the bare wooden walls, lending a homey atmosphere to our simple dwelling.

MORNING PRAYER

I threw the covers back and slid to the wood floor, pulling the braided carpet under my knees to cushion them. I leaned over the bed and bowed my head. "Lord Jesus, thank You for waking me up. I love this early morning, intimate time with You," I said, quietly.

My first thoughts were of home and kin. Love and gratitude poured from me for my church family and for all of the spiritual pioneers, both past and present, who refused to quit, courageous enough to press on toward the final frontier of God's ultimate purpose.

Frontier Town is more than a vision to me; it is a spiritual reality, I thought, *a place where we are forced to grow up in God.*

SPIRIT WIND

A DESPERATE PLEA

"Lord," I pleaded, with passionate desperation. "Please wake Your people up; so many of us are asleep in complacency and indifference. We have become satisfied with the status quo and have succumbed to comfort and convenience. We want pleasure more than You. We need revived.

"We are more concerned with the opinions of men than what You desire and demand, Jesus. We have settled into a state of selfish consumption. We want Your power and miracles so we can consume them upon ourselves. We ask You for Your favor, but our motives are wrong. Our hearts are not set on advancing Your Kingdom; we just want to be blessed ourselves."[1]

Paul's warning to the Christians of his own era shouted in my spirit.

"Remember our history, friends, and be warned. All our ancestors were led by the providential Cloud and taken miraculously through the Sea. They went through the waters, in a baptism like ours, as Moses led them from enslaving death to salvation life. They all ate and drank identical food and drink, meals provided daily by God. They drank from the Rock, God's fountain for them that stayed with them wherever they were. And the Rock was Christ. But just experiencing God's wonder and grace didn't seem to mean much — most of them were defeated by temptation during the hard times in the desert, and God was not pleased.

The same thing could happen to us. We must be on guard so that we never get caught up in wanting our own way as they did. And we must not turn our religion into a circus as they did — "First the people partied, then they threw a dance." We must not be sexually promiscuous — they paid for that, remember, with twenty-three thousand deaths in one day! We must never try to get Christ to serve us instead of us serving him; they tried it, and God launched an epidemic of poisonous snakes. We must be careful not to stir up discontent; discontent destroyed them.

These are all warning markers — DANGER! — in our history books, written down so that we don't repeat their mistakes. Our positions in the story are parallel — they at the beginning, we at the end - and we are just as capable of messing up as they were. Don't be so naïve and self-confident. You're not exempt. You could fall flat on your face as easily as anyone else. Forget about self-confidence; it's useless. Cultivate God-confidence.

No test or temptation that comes your way is beyond the course of what others have had to face. All you need to remember is that God will never let you down; he'll never let you be pushed past your limit; he'll always be there to help you come through it" (First Corinthians 10:1-13, MSG).

PRAYING IN THE SPIRIT

My heart ached for the church as I interceded with impassioned groans, at times unable to find words adequate to express my thoughts. Sounds rose up from within my spirit that I knew originated in the heart of the Father.[2]

"We succumb to so many temptations, Jesus: idolatry, pride, sexual immorality," I confessed. "We continually test You to see just how much we can get away with. We display a blatant disregard for Your holiness. We grumble and complain, bringing shame and disgrace upon Your family and household. Forgive us, Jesus," I sobbed. "Please, forgive us.

"Oh God, we have fallen prey to the very thing Paul cautioned us to avoid. His warning is so appropriate. The end of the ages has come upon us, Lord! There isn't much time left. Open our eyes; let Your church see that the end of the ages has arrived."

THE WORST SIN OF ALL

Then an awful realization struck me. *The worst sin of all would be to die in the wilderness and fail to fulfill God's purpose and destiny; to stop short of the goal.*

"Lord," I pleaded in fervent intercession for my generation and the remaining few still to come. "Don't let our bodies be scattered in the wilderness of unfulfilled promise like those of our rebellious forefathers. Don't let our lives be wasted on petty, selfish pursuits. Oh Father, we long to see the words of Your prophets come to pass and the mission of the Savior fully accomplished.

SPIRIT WIND

"Shake us in our boots. Lead us like spiritual pioneers into unconquered territory. Shape us into an army of end-time warriors; a new breed, powerfully anointed by You, walking in Your power. Enable us to be reapers of the final harvest."

LET ME BE A WITNESS

I turned from my bed and crawled across the floor to where Timothy lay sleeping. My spirit was totally engaged in an agonizing, invisible battle. The thought of even the possibility that I might fail to complete my assignment was terrifying. I laid my hands on Timothy's sleeping frame and continued to pray with hopefulness.

"Lord," I pleaded, with all the urgency and sincerity I could muster. "I want my life be an encouragement to Tim not to stop short of his destiny. I don't want to be known as a quitter. Let my witness and legacy be one of courage, endurance and unfailing faith. Help me to finish well, Jesus."

I breathed a final request, "**Please don't allow me to be among those who set out to follow You and settle for less than the total accomplishment of Your will.** Let me be an end-time warrior, a forever pilgrim, until I rest in Your presence."

PRAYER MAKES A DIFFERENCE

I'm not sure how long I prayed. Light was just beginning to filter into the room from outside when I finally extinguished the lantern. Tim woke to the sound of the shuffling blankets as I made my bunk.

"Come on, Tim," I said. "Let's get some breakfast at the café."

"Funny thing," he said as he straightened his bed and gathered his things. "I had this dream last night about spiritual warfare. The phrase kept repeating over and over in my dream, 'Wage a good warfare, wage a good warfare!' I could feel courage and strength rising up within my spirit.[3]

"I feel so encouraged today. I just want to serve God with all of my heart. My life belongs to Him!" he said. "I am determined to win with His help. I

146

will fulfill all the prophecies and promises He has spoken over me. I refuse to settle for anything less. Nothing, or no one, will hold me back."

I smiled a reassuring smile and uttered under my breath, "Thank You, Lord, for answered prayer."

"There's a place I want to show you today, Tim, if we get some free time," I said. "It's probably the most important thing you will ever learn here in Frontier Town. It will help you for the rest of your life as a spiritual pilgrim and end-time warrior. I know that you're going to love this, Tim, as much as I do!"

Chapter Nineteen

TRAVELING LIGHT

We hurried down the boardwalk to the *Koinonia* Café. The aroma of freshly falling rain perfumed the atmosphere with a scintillating, amorous ambiance. Its jasmine-like sweetness brought thoughts of springtime and life to Frontier Town. *It's just plain, downright wonderful to be alive,* I thought, drinking in the fresh, revitalizing atmosphere.

"It really is an incredible day," I said, punching Tim in the ribs jovially. "What an amazing age we're blessed to enjoy. Do you realize just how privileged we are to be pioneers right now? We're living at the end of the ages!"

"Yep," he chirped back. "Just the thought of it excites me! I can't wait to see what God will do next."

SINGING FOR BREAKFAST

We entered the café to find the entire crowd singing with fantastic enthusiasm. **"Imagine this," I exclaimed, pointing in the direction of the coffee urn, "people actually singing at breakfast. What a great place this is!"**

We filled our cups and found two seats together at the counter. The waiters were busy passing out fresh bread. We hungrily grabbed our share, savoring the rich flavor and texture of the huge pieces.

"It's the same bread they always serve here at the café," Tim said, crunching a huge chunk of crust between his teeth. "I'll never forget the first time I tasted it. But this time it has a wonderfully enhanced flavor."

"This is great stuff," I shouted back, over the singing. "I'm full already! This is the most satisfying bread in the whole world."

FREE TIME IN FRONTIER TOWN

"Did you see any sign of Spirit Wind?" I asked between gulps of coffee. I had the distinct sense that Tim and I had been given a day off.

"Sure didn't," he said. "I wonder what's up."

"I think the Lord has granted us a day of rest and relaxation, Tim. We get to choose whatever we want to do here in Frontier Town."

"Really? That's cool!" he said, setting his cup down with a thud on the counter.

Slurping the last dregs of my coffee, I nudged him and said, "Come on, partner. I want to show you a surprise. Let's you and I go exploring together right here on Main Street."

We waved goodbye to our fellow pioneers at the café and stepped through the door into the warm morning sunshine. "It's stopped raining," I said, looking down at the sun reflecting off of the puddles on Main Street.

FOLLOW ME

"Follow me!" I directed, with the enthusiasm of a tour guide leading his client to new places of discovery. I turned left and headed up the boardwalk past the partially painted two-story building and the rich green lawn of the schoolhouse.

The sound of our boots on the planking was music to my pioneer heart. *We're on our way again,* I thought with great delight. *What a thrilling life. We are pioneers in God's Kingdom, end-time warriors set free to roam and discover God's plans and purposes.* I just wanted to keep on singing. My heart was full of melodies to the Lord.

Paul was busily sorting the morning mail when we strolled by the General's Store. "Not now, Tim. We'll come back for the mail later," I said.

I slowed my pace a little when we passed the silo. I could feel the gentle, flickering response of my spirit as we walked by. *I wonder if Timothy senses what I do?* I thought. Then I reminded myself, *He must be feeling something! This is The Secret Place and only those with genuine thirst for God ever discover its existence. I don't know anyone thirstier than Tim.*

THE STORAGE SHED

I stopped abruptly in front of the half-story, windowless shed. Timothy never suspected I would lead him to this building. He kept right on walking until he suddenly realized I wasn't beside him anymore. He turned and looked at me quizzically. "What could be so exciting about a windowless storage shed?" he asked.

I didn't try to explain. Sometimes there's just something about personal experience that words can't adequately clarify.

"Things aren't what they seem to be here in Frontier Town, remember? Wait till you see what's inside," I said, intentionally trying to provoke his curiosity. "The Lord brought me here last night while you were sleeping. He insisted that I leave some things inside this building. He promised that He would take care of them for me."

OPENING THE LOCK

I grasped the cylindrical combination lock in my left hand and lifted it perpendicular to the door so that I could clearly see the dials. Instead of numbers, each of the three dials contained a group of symbols on its circumference. I spun the top dial, examining each of the icons.

What kind of code is this? I thought, struggling not to appear stupid in front of Timothy. *I'm sorry now that I didn't pay closer attention when Jesus opened it last night. All of my years of education and study are of no help to me now.* I panicked, fighting off embarrassment, and fumbled with the lock, pretending it was jammed. *This makes no sense to me at all. I can't decipher this code.*

Then I heard His voice within me. "Relax," the Holy Spirit whispered, ever so softly. **"Let your heart determine the combination. It requires a spiritual equation to open this lock and grant you entrance.** Allow Me to reveal the secret code that must always be used to open this door."

I spun the first dial again. Refusing to rely on my ability or knowledge, this time I focused on His inner presence, trusting the Holy Spirit to reveal the correct symbol. Nothing happened! I spun it a third time, feeling like a freshman high school student who forgot his combination and couldn't open his locker.

I wonder if Timothy has detected my incompetence, I thought, wincing with stress. *I must believe. The Spirit has promised me the combination. Faith is required here!* The moment the thought passed through my mind I felt the dial click and stop.

I moved my thumb down to the second wheel and turned it slowly. "I hope this works a second time." Instantly, the dial stopped; a definite clicking sound signaled the right symbol. Then it struck me. *The combination is faith, hope, and love.* I excitedly turned the last dial and the lock fell open in my hand.

"Did you see the combination, Tim?" I asked.

"I did," he replied, "but the symbols make no sense to me."

"It takes faith," I explained. "Remember, it's faith first and then hope, but the last and greatest part of the combination is love. Without faith, hope and love you can't open this lock."

WATCH YOUR HEAD!

I swung the door open, bent low to avoid the doorframe, and crawled into the darkened storage shed. "Follow me, and watch your head!" I warned, but it was too late.

"Ouch! Owey!" Tim cried, as his head struck the top of the frame. "I did it again! When will I learn not to be so hasty? This is gonna leave a bruise," he moaned, rubbing his forehead. He slammed the door closed angrily.

I didn't say a word. I wanted him to discover the purpose for this building on his own. Narrow lines of light fell into the room through the cracked weathered seams in the flat roof. Dust particles swam in the hazy glow; visible in mid-air, they looked like microscopic bugs in water.

"It's impossible to stand up straight; the ceiling's just too low," Tim complained. "I feel like I'm in my grandmother's attic." The moment his eyes grew accustomed to the darkness, the enigma of the oddly shaped building on Main Street in Frontier Town was revealed.

GOD'S ATTIC

The entire room was filled with suitcases and trunks of all sizes and shapes. There appeared to be no particular order or arrangement to the conglomeration of baggage. Stacked in random piles extending from the dirt floor all the way to the flat ceiling, each bag was still within easy reach.

Canvas bags and sacks were scattered about among the disarray of stored items. Dust covered everything. It was clearly obvious that the things deposited here had not been touched for some time. Some items seemed to be very old, presumably left behind by spiritual pioneers who passed through Frontier Town in a former age who never reclaimed their baggage.

Always remember that love covers a multitude of sins.

Tim reached out to open the metal clasp on a nearby suitcase, intending to examine its contents. "Don't touch that!" I quickly scolded. "That doesn't belong to you. You have no business nosing around in someone else's baggage. How would you like it if someone rooted around in yours?"

"Sorry," he apologized sheepishly, "I didn't mean any harm."

"That's just the problem, Tim," I explained. "No one means any harm when they open up someone else's baggage, but it always ends up exposing things that are private, personal and embarrassing.

"Trouble is, some pioneers seem to enjoy exposing other people's dirty laundry. It can get really ugly, and the worldly folks seem to delight in publishing abroad what is exposed. It's so grievous.

153

"Remember the last and most important part of the combination that opened the lock and gave us entrance into this storage shed? Love, Tim. It's love! Always remember that love covers a multitude of sins."[1]

IS THERE ROOM FOR MINE?

The full impact of why the storage shed existed on Main Street hit Tim right between the eyes. It provided a place to store the unwanted baggage of every spiritual pioneer who ever passed through Frontier Town. They all left their burdens and failures stored here in this windowless shed, never to be reclaimed. Only foolish and unkind fellow pioneers would dare to open the luggage and expose their brothers' and sisters' past sins and mistakes.

Tim closed the latch on the suitcase expeditiously. "Thank God I didn't open it," he uttered, breathing a sigh of relief. He looked at me with hurt in his eyes and said, "I wonder if I could leave some of my things here too?"

"Sure," I replied. "That's the unique thing about this shed. It keeps changing size to accommodate whatever is left here. It's big enough to hold everybody's baggage."

I pointed to the rather large collection of burgundy suitcases and spoke in a broken voice. "Why don't you just store your stuff next to mine, Tim?" The moment I said the words, gratitude overwhelmed me. Tears of thankfulness coursed down my cheek, unseen in the dim light of the storage shed, and fell to the earthen floor.

"I'll make a deal with you, partner," I said. "Don't ever open my bags and I promise I will never open yours."

"I wouldn't think of it," he replied with genuine love and respect.

RELEASE

I crawled toward the back of the shed, leaving Tim alone for a while. I knew he needed some privacy to get rid of the baggage he had been carrying for a lifetime. I sensed that some of it had to do with his father, but I refused to let my imagination get carried away. *It's between him and You, Lord,* I affirmed.

154

Finally, he appeared out of the shadows, his face glowing with lighthearted relief. He moved through the piles of luggage with an unencumbered ease.

"All set?" I asked.

"Oh, yes," he replied. "I sure am glad to get rid of all that stuff. It's so much easier to move now. I'll never try to carry that again. I've laid it down once and for all. I sure hope no one else opens it up. It would break my heart!"

"Me, too, Tim," I said. "It would break mine, too!"

THE PASSAGEWAY TO INTIMACY

We knelt together at the back corner of the storage shed peering into the narrow, rectangular wood tunnel. A mist filled its entire length, obscuring the far end of the corridor.

"How far to the other side?" Tim asked.

"It's about thirty-five feet. That seems a long way through the mist, but it only takes seconds to get there. Come on," I said excitedly. "This is what I've been waiting to show you! It's The Secret Place, and this is the easiest way to get in. When you leave your baggage behind in this storage shed you can get into His presence much more easily."

PRESSING INTO HIS PRESENCE

Bent low on hands and knees, we committed ourselves to the mystical passageway. A holy presence filled the mysterious tunnel. With each crawling inch, we became more aware of the awesome presence of the living God. Pressing steadily ahead with fearful reverence, Tim and I reached the end of the passageway and crawled out into the circular spaciousness of the silo.

The light from a single lantern hanging above the stone well in the center of the room engulfed us. Tim froze in place, awestruck at the sight of the two incredibly strong warrior angels standing like sentries guarding the well. He stood agape, unable to speak.

"Tim," I said, in a muted tone. "This is The Well of His Presence. This is where I come to walk with the Lord. **There are mysteries and secrets here that** only those who know how can draw up from the heart of God. This is The Secret Place that only determined spiritual pioneers with desperate hearts ever discover.

"The Lord has instructed me to tell my fellow pioneers about the well and to encourage them to seek it often. You're the first one I've actually brought here. We had to enter through the only passageway on Main Street. The only way in and out of Frontier Town is through the well itself."

MEET MY FRIENDS

Tim, still awestruck by the angels, managed to nod his head in acknowledgment.

"Oh, I'm sorry. Forgive me," I said apologetically. "Let me introduce you to Gillar and Mannor. They are two of the angels who guard the revelation from The Well of His Presence. They have been my guardians and companions since I began this journey."

Timothy, regaining his composure, bowed his head in a respectful nod of greeting.

Gillar spoke with masculine strength. "Welcome Timothy, loved of God. Welcome to The Well of His Presence."

Instantly, Tim was gone.

Mannor stepped up to the well to arrange a new vessel, carefully placing it near the side of the entrance. I knew immediately that it was intended for Timothy. He had disappeared into the well to walk with Jesus. A new revelation was being drawn up out of the depths of God's infinite wisdom and knowledge in The Secret Place.

Gillar smiled at me. "Well done," he said, and then went about his work, keeping constant vigilance.

Another vessel near where I stood was almost filled to the brim. The surface of the water rippled as though some unseen person were pouring more liquid into it. The words "Frontier Town" were inscribed on the outer surface of the clay water pot.

"It's mine," I gasped, "and it's almost full."

GET SOME REST!

The well disappeared from view. The angel was gone and the holy glow vanished. I found myself standing alone on the boardwalk in front of the silo on Main Street in broad daylight.

There's an unusual restfulness in town today, I thought. *I noticed it back at the café this morning. My goodness, I don't even know what day it is. I've lost all track of time since I arrived in Frontier Town. I'll bet it must be the Sabbath, the appointed day of rest. I guess I'll mosey on over to the post office and then head back to the bunkhouse to sit and rest a while. Sure do have a lot to meditate on.*

Mail in hand, I walked back to the bunkhouse and moved my captain's chair from inside onto the deck. I sat down and tilted onto the rear legs. Leaning back against the front wall of the bunkhouse, I settled into the narrow band of shade.

After a while, I plucked a tall stalk of wild grass growing up between the cracks of the boardwalk beside me and stuck it into the right side of my mouth. It tasted sweet. *This is the life*, I thought, contentedly watching the lazy activity on Main Street until the sun was low in the western sky.

SUNDAY NIGHT ON MAIN STREET

Every now and then a new pioneer arrived in town. I would tip my hat and greet them with a genuine "Howdy partner, good to meet you!" I knew from my own experience what incredible discoveries were in store for them.

After several hours of reverie, I went back to the café for a bit of refreshment and a chat with friends, then headed off to bed.

Timothy was still gone. He had been in The Well of His Presence since midday. I knew the Lord was speaking to him about destiny, purpose and end-time strategies. But what really delighted my soul the most was that Timothy had discovered The Secret Place. He was enjoying intimacy with his heavenly Father, and that is what he was created for.

I tumbled into bed with a grateful heart. "Good night, Lord," I mumbled, drifting off to sleep. A deep satisfaction swept over me. I knew I had accomplished part of my God-given assignment in life. I had led one of God's spiritual pilgrims to The Well of His Presence.

Chapter Twenty

THE SALOON

Timothy sat straight up in bed. "Can't they show some respect? We're trying to sleep in here!" he complained in a loud voice, hoping that whoever was making the obnoxious racket might hear him.

"What's going on?" I asked gruffly, not very happy about being disturbed myself.

"I don't know!" he said in frustration, rising from his bed and putting his ear to the wall on my side of the bunkhouse. "It's coming from next door; sounds like a party going on over there."

He tumbled back into bed, and for about a half hour we tossed and turned in a fruitless attempt to get back to sleep. Finally, I sat up and angrily grabbed my sword. "Come on, Tim, I'm going next door to see if I can quiet down the neighbors!"

Better take all my things, I thought at the last second. *By the sound of that crowd, you never know what might happen. I need to be prepared for anything.* I hastily retrieved my eye salve and identification letter from the night stand and shoved them into my shepherd's bag. We stomped down the boardwalk a few paces to the swinging doors of the adjacent building.

A RUCKUS IN THE SALOON

What a den of iniquity, I thought in disgust. An evil presence exuded from the building. The entire three-story structure was lit up like a Las Vegas casino.

159

SPIRIT WIND

The light flashing from the upper windows reminded me of the gaudy, fluorescent glow of a cheap neon sign. I could hear footsteps above us on the balcony, and a woman moaned in a seductive tone. Mind-numbing music filled the interior of the first floor and inebriated patrons yelled back and forth at each other with obnoxious, slurred speech.

We threw open the swinging doors and pounced into the room like Wyatt Earp and his deputy. "I've had enough!" I shouted, with intimidating authority. "We just want some sleep. We want peace and quiet here in Frontier Town and we're going to get it even if we have to use force!"

A DEN OF INIQUITY

The repulsive sight looked like a scene from an x-rated movie. In the far corner, several teenagers were huddled around a table blatantly injecting heroin into their arms. A group of men were gathered at the bar slurping drinks and making rude, obscene comments and gestures to the barmaid. Stacks of pornographic magazines and pictures were piled on a table. Several people were eagerly devouring their contents with a glazed look of lust on their faces.

Women scantily attired in seductive negligees pranced about flaunting themselves unashamedly. They merchandised their bodies like hardware available for the right amount of money, beckoning the male clientele to follow them upstairs.

The abhorrent sight was nauseating. *If you love God, you don't fit here*, I thought in disgust. Almost every type of fleshy pursuit was evident. Prostitution, pornography, drunkenness, drugs, uncleanness, lewdness and revelry were encouraged and condoned.[1] There was such hatred and anger underlying it all. Blatant rebellion infected the clientele with mesmerizing stupidity.[2] What really provoked me were the demonic spirits of destruction and murder that motivated the unruly crowd. Righteous indignation rose up within me.

JUDGMENT OR MERCY

"Judgment is what we need here," I determined, reaching for my sword. "Let's clean house, Timothy!" I shouted, angrily.[3]

160

I was about to draw my sword when a teenaged girl brushed past me. She had a boyish look about her. Her brownish-black hair was cut into short stubby curls close to her scalp and it bounced like miniature springs when she walked. I guessed her to be about fourteen or fifteen.

Her ears looked like pin cushions. Two cheap silver studs ornamented her pierced nostrils. But it was her eyes that really told me the story. They were big, round, dark and haunting. An aching desperation lay just beneath their surface in the pool of her soul. She masked her hidden pain by an outer bravado, but I could tell that she was desperately crying out for someone to love her.

Jesus didn't give me this sword so I could kill people with it. I'm supposed to minister healing.

I froze in place, providentially diverted from my vengeful pursuit of judgment. I was incapacitated by her pain. *She's someone's daughter. How did she end up in this awful place?* I thought, struggling with the compassion welling up inside me. My heart broke.

COMING TO MY SENSES

I watched as she made her way unnoticed through the crowd. She took a seat at a table in the far corner of the room next to the lone figure of a middle-aged man. **I stared in shock. "It's Jesus! She's sitting at the table with Jesus!"**

A tidal wave of guilt flooded over me. *How could I be so blind? In my anger, I've lost all sense of why I'm here in Frontier Town. God didn't call me here for peace and quiet. This is not a vacation in spiritual paradise. I'm here for training as an end-time warrior. I'm supposed to be an agent of mercy, not judgment.*

I trembled at the thought that I had almost used the sword of the Lord to destroy others. *Jesus didn't give me this sword so I could kill people with it. I'm supposed to minister healing. I feel like Peter when he cut off the soldier's ear in the garden of Gethsemane.[4] I really meant to inflict damage, just like he did. I can't believe what's in my heart.* "Thank God I didn't draw the sword," I said, sucking putrid air into my lungs.

SPIRIT WIND

THE PHARISEE

I watched Jesus minister to the young woman with loving kindness. His demeanor brought me to my spiritual senses. *Why didn't it occur to me before? This is the very place where Jesus would show up in Frontier Town. Here is where the need is. I've been acting like a Pharisee. I should be full of compassion instead of judging these sinners. Jesus rebuked the Pharisees in Israel for my kind of behavior.*

The recollection of His words burned like acid in my conscience. *"Those who are well have no need of a physician, but those who are sick. But go and learn what this means: 'I desire mercy and not sacrifice.' For I did not come to call the righteous, but sinners, to repentance"* (Matthew 9:12-13).

"I'm no different than the self-righteous Pharisees of Jesus' day," I mumbled, distressed by my disgraceful attitude. "You can include me in the mob of religious rock throwers who tried to kill the woman caught in adultery. Jesus told that crowd of snobs, *'He that is without sin among you, let him throw a stone at her first.'* "⁵

The truth of His indictment cut through my self-righteous delusion like an armor-piercing bullet plunging into my heart. I stumbled across the room and looked with humiliation into Jesus' eyes.

"Jesus, I'm so sorry. Is there any hope for me? Please change my heart, Lord!"

He smiled with reassuring mercy. "It's all right, son! This is basic training. But when the real test comes, I want you to be ready!"

COMPASSIONATE EYES

"You made a crucial mistake," He continued. "You failed to use the gift I gave you months ago. It's the one thing that will help you to see others as I see them, no matter how sinful they may be."

"What is it, Lord?" I asked.

"It's in your shepherd's bag, son. Don't you remember? It's the eye salve I gave you months ago in the Hidden Kingdom."⁶

I shook my head in embarrassment. "I guess I was so angry when I came in here that I completely forgot about it."

I reached into my shepherd's bag and removed the small milk-glass jar. **Dipping my finger into the supernatural ointment, I applied a small amount of the pure cream to my eyes. The results were immediate.** My spiritual perspective was transformed. Soothing mercy and comforting compassion filled my spirit.

I opened my eyes and looked around the room. "You're right, Lord. Everyone here looks different to me now. I know they haven't changed; I'm the one who's different. My heart feels pure. I don't have the desire to judge them anymore; I want to rescue them instead! All I can see is Your blood shed for them. Your blood conquers all sin, Jesus."

"Now you understand My heart," Jesus said. "Don't be overcome by evil. Overcome evil with good.[7] Remember the spiritual warriors' motto: *To Conquer, To Love, To Redeem.* Hide it in your heart, son. Don't ever forget it!"

"I won't, Sir," I replied.

Chapter Twenty-One

COMPASSION ON MAIN STREET

*W*here did Timothy go? I thought, anxiously searching the smoke-filled saloon for any sign of him; but he was nowhere in sight. *He's got to be here somewhere; I'm sure he wouldn't leave without me. Maybe he's upstairs. Well, wherever he went, I'm sure he's learning something. It's obvious that this disturbance is working out for our benefit.*[1]

I turned my attention back to our table and listened attentively to the conversation between Jesus and the young woman across from us. She hung on every word He said with the intensity of a sick patient desperate for healing.

AMAZING GRACE

"Who is he?" Jesus asked.

Her eyes opened wide in panic. She looked away trying in vain to hide from Him. "He knows. Oh God, He knows," she whispered.

"Who is he?" Jesus said a second time, without a trace of condemnation.

A tear seeped from the corner of her eye. She wiped it in desperation, but it was too late. Her pain spilled onto the table. She pounded her clenched fists against it until her knuckles turned blood-red. Raw, vengeful hatred spewed out of her like venom from a rattlesnake, soiling the already poisonous atmosphere with her vileness. When her anger was finally spent, her head dropped onto the crumpled tablecloth with a thump. She wrapped her arms around her face and convulsed in wrenching sobs until she could move no longer.

She spoke so softly I could barely hear her voice. "Jared!" she said. The name spilled out into her tangled arms. "His name is Jared."

"You loved him, didn't you?" Jesus asked.

"I thought so, then..." she replied.

The scorching seconds of her silence seemed like hours to me. It was excruciating. I wanted to say something, to put the words in her mouth, to ease the emotional pressure building like steam in a boiling kettle. *Do something!* I thought, glaring at Jesus. He just waited patiently, silently, for her to speak. He waited to let her say the words that would set her free.

She raised her head. Her eyes were swollen and bloodshot. "Yes, I loved him. I still love him!" Her weary tears drained down her pale white cheeks and fell to the table like broken dreams.

"And the child?" Jesus said, tenderly.

"He's gone... Oh!" she sobbed. Her head fell back on the table. "My son!" she moaned in terrible grief. "I had to, I just had to! They took him away from me in the hospital! I only held him once. Only once!" She wept again, draining the deep reservoir of her pain, her arms rocking with the aching emptiness that only a mother who has lost a child can know.

"I hate him! I love him, but I hate him! I'm so confused. I can never forgive him for what he did to me. He told me he loved me. The night I gave myself to him he promised that he would love me forever.

"It was so beautiful while it lasted, but somehow inside I knew it wasn't right. My life is over now. I ran away from home. My parents don't know where I am. I've been gone for six months. I finally found this place. They gave me a small room on the third floor. I sell myself to pay for it and for the little bit of food they provide."

Jesus was on His feet, standing beside the young girl and gently stroking her short hair. He reached down to lift her chin from the table and turned her head toward Him. Kneeling down beside her, He looked directly into her eyes.

"It's over, Charlene," He said. "Look around! Do you see anyone accusing you?"

Her eyes darted around the room. "There's no one, Lord," she said, staring into His honest face.

"Neither do I," He replied.

THE MIRACLE

The miraculous transformation happened before my eyes. Her devastation turned to hope. A tiny spark lit up her eyes. A healing cry of release sprang from deep inside her. She threw her arms around Jesus in an embrace of freedom. What an awesome sight – Jesus kneeling on the dirty floor of the bar room and Charlene with her head buried in His neck.

They were locked in an embrace of healing mercy and compassion. When she reluctantly released her grip and raised her head, her eyes were full of life and hope. A smile of innocence graced her countenance.

Jesus' shoulder was wet from her tears. He looked reassuringly at her and cupped her cheeks in His hands. "Charlene," He said, "your son is doing just fine. I have watched over him. His parents love him like he is their very own. Your sacrifice has filled their emptiness and removed their pain. They are so happy.

"He's just fine, honey!" He said stroking her cheek. "He's just fine! And someday you will see him again. I promise you! Listen to Me." He spoke in a firm, Fatherly tone. "There is something you must do now."

"What is it?" she asked. "I'll do anything, Jesus!"

"I want you to forgive yourself…and I want you to forgive Jared."

An instant of anger distorted her face, but just as quickly it dissolved into peaceful surrender. "I will, Lord!" she sighed in relief. "I forgive him right now! I'm so sorry I let you down, Jesus. I disappointed everyone, especially my mom and dad. They're so hurt."

"Forgive yourself, daughter. It's over now! Your heavenly Father can heal every wound!"

HOMEWARD BOUND

"I need to go," she said. "I have to go home!"

He smiled and reached over playfully to touch one of the dangling earrings on her left ear. He gave it a light flick with His finger. It struck the silver one beneath it and sounded a crisp cheerful tone, like a miniature sleigh bell. "Yes, daughter," He said. **"You must go home, but know this. You are greatly loved. I will never leave you or forsake you."**

Charlene jumped from the table and bounced through the inattentive crowd with a vivacious spring in her step. Her youthful innocence and joy had been restored.

We watched her until she reached the swinging door. Just before she stepped through it, she turned and waved back with a delightful, carefree smile. "Thank You, Jesus!" she shouted across the room above all the noise. "I'll never be the same again!" She disappeared into the night on Main Street.

MOTIVATED BY COMPASSION

I pulled my chair closer to the table and lowered my head slightly to avoid distractions. "I need some time to process this evening's events and let the full significance of what happened work in me," I said. "I feel like I've been at Jacob's pottery shop, Lord. I'm as broken down as a piece of clay that's been kneaded, poked and pushed until every last lump of resistance has been pounded into submission. I'm emotionally pulverized. I can feel the heat of the kiln in my soul."

"I'm blessed to hear you say that," He replied, "because I brought you here to teach you a critical lesson. It's one of the most important keys to being a successful end-time warrior. You must be motivated by compassion!"

Jesus spoke with complete candor. "I am gracious and full of compassion. I am slow to anger and great in mercy. I am good to all and My tender mercies are over all My works.[2] When I walked the earth in My flesh I preached the gospel of the Kingdom and healed every kind of sickness and disease. I often traveled many miles just to heal one person.[3]

"It was compassion that moved Me to feed a multitude with a few loaves and fishes. That day I healed everyone who was sick.[4] It was because of My great compassion that I healed the leper and raised the widow's dead son at the city gate in Nain.[5] I even wept openly at the tomb of My friend Lazarus.[6] There are so many tormented, wounded and sick people, entire cities of scattered sheep wandering unprotected and vulnerable without a shepherd. At times, I'm overcome with compassion.

"Long ago I stood on a hillside overlooking Jerusalem. *'O Jerusalem, Jerusalem,'* I cried. *'The one who kills the prophets and stones those who are sent to her! How often I wanted to gather your children together, as a hen gathers her brood under her wings, but you were not willing! See! Your house is left to you desolate; and assuredly, I say to you, you shall not see Me until the time comes when you say, "Blessed is He who comes in the name of the Lord!"'* [Luke 13:34-35]. My compassion still burns white-hot for Israel, My chosen people."

BE LIKE ME

"You must be slow to anger!" He said, with emphasis. "That is why the eye salve is so important. Without it you will not treat others with kindness. Anoint your eyes with the salve often, so that you may see![7] **I want all of My servants to be like Me: compassionate warriors, dispensers of mercy, an army of healers.**"

Charlene's face flashed before my eyes as He spoke. A tinge of conviction pricked my conscience. "Lord, that's my prayer and desire. Fill me with Your compassion. Let Your heart burn within me."

"The Holy Spirit will fulfill your request, if you let Him," He answered.

MY FIRST TEST

Jesus left the table and disappeared into the crowd. I sat alone in the corner of the saloon recording the events of the evening in my field manual. Just as I closed my handbook, the chair next to me slid out and someone sat down. *He must have been watching me and had the courtesy to wait until I finished,* I thought in appreciation.

SPIRIT WIND

I looked up from my textbook and twitched with an uneasy awkwardness. One of the guys I had observed earlier reading a pornographic magazine was sitting beside me. He was an older man, kind of *Where's Waldo?* indistinct, who could easily blend into a crowd without drawing attention to himself. He wore his wedding band on his right hand. His eyes had a hypnotized glaze and his movements were indecisive. He fumbled around like someone drugged with a sedative.

He spoke to me in clandestine tones and kept scoping the room suspiciously to see if anyone was watching. "I desperately need help!" he pleaded, with embarrassment written all over his face. "I just can't shake this horrible addiction to sex. My wife has no idea what I'm going through. She'd be devastated if she ever found out. I don't know who to turn to. I'm in torment! I've tried, but I can't break out of this prison. I've been watching you ever since you came in tonight. There's something different about you. I felt compelled to seek your advice. Please, can you help me?"

ANGRY FOR THE RIGHT REASON

His confession infuriated me. I grasped my sword and yanked the glistening blade into the open. Anger exploded inside of me, but this time my rage wasn't aimed at this person. I was incensed by the insidious tactics of the enemy that held him captive with such malevolent tenacity that they were destroying his marriage and his life. I felt compassion for his imprisoned soul.

"Yes! I can help!" I said, sweeping my sword over his head inches above his scalp. He dodged the blade, but refused to retreat.

I thrust my weapon at the invisible enemy, chopping away at his sinister lies with dogged determination. "There is a way to escape; there's Someone Who can set you free."[8]

I plunged my sword deep into the heart of the enemy. "Someone loves you so much that He gave His life to rescue you." I shouted, over the mocking bar room cacophony.[9] *'The wages of sin is death, but the gift of God is eternal life through Jesus Christ our Lord.'*[10] Jesus can set you free from this prison, and even better, He can give you eternal life."

"I need Jesus," he stammered. "I need Him now! I'm possessed with lust. Every waking moment, I'm consumed with this obsession. Help me!" he cried. "Set me free, Jesus!"

A shrieking scream erupted from his mouth. The terrified demon fled from the name of Jesus like a burglar caught in the act, fleeing the scene of the crime.

I watched with joy as the Holy Spirit restored the redeemed man. His eyes grew clear and focused. His perception returned to clear conscience keenness. He reached for his ring, slid it from his finger and transferred it to his left hand. His movements were precise and decided. He was transformed, a new creature in Christ Jesus, set free by the power of God.[11]

SURRENDER!

I lifted my sword above my head and pointed heavenward in victory. "The sword of the Lord," I declared. "God means what He says. What He says goes. His powerful Word is sharp as a surgeon's scalpel, cutting through everything, whether doubt or defense, laying us open to listen and obey. Nothing and no one is impervious to God's Word. We can't get away from it – no matter what.[12]

"The enemy must surrender to its authority," I announced, looking around the room at all of the people in the saloon. Every trace of self-righteous anger within me was gone. "I came here for a fight," I said, "but instead I learned compassion.[13] Things aren't what they seem to be here in Frontier Town!"

I sheathed my sword and shoved my way through the throng of patrons toward the exit. The doors slapped back and forth behind me.

The noise is still as obnoxious, I thought. *The crowd parties on.*

IT'S JUST A FAÇADE

I stepped down from the boardwalk onto the clay surface of Main Street and glanced up through the left window into the saloon. What I saw stunned me. Since I had arrived in Frontier Town, someone had painted a single word on the window pane in large block letters. The black paint was still wet and some excess ran down from the bottom point of the 'N'.

"TOWN," I read, bewildered. "What's the rest?" I asked, jerking my head toward the right window.

"JAIL," I blurted out in astonishment.

"Town Jail! This isn't a saloon; it's the Town Jail," I said, dumbfounded.

The door flew open and Timothy stepped out of the jailhouse. "Whew!" he said in exhaustion. "What a harvest of souls in there! I think we've been spending too much time at the *Koinonia* Café and not enough time ministering to the prisoners in the saloon. This is where the harvest is."

A TROUBLED SLEEP

We lay in our bunks for a long time unable to sleep, not because of the noise, but because our hearts ached with compassion for the prisoners locked in their personal cells of pain and sin next door.

"Set the captives free, Lord," I prayed. "Use us to set the captives free."

A troubled sleep finally came!

Chapter Twenty-Two

FORMING THE POSSE

I bounded out of bed with zealous enthusiasm. "Quick, Tim," I ordered, "gather your stuff. We've got work to do!"

He hit the floor running. "I'll be ready in a flash," he said, tucking his blanket under the mattress at the bottom of the bed.

We made up our bunks and scurried around the room attacking the cleaning chores like busy maids in a five-star hotel. Tim even ran his finger across his desk to check for dust.

"I think we've got it," he said, scanning the room like a marine officer inspecting the barracks. We closed the door behind us, fully satisfied that any future occupant would find the room ready. We both knew we would not return.

We hurried down Main Street. Timothy turned presumptuously to enter the Town Jail. I grabbed his belt and pulled him back just in time. "Whoa, partner!" I declared. "We've got to let the others know! We'll come back here later." He turned away with a reluctant pout and we continued along Main Street.

TRAVEL LIGHT

When we passed the storage shed, Tim patted me on the back gratefully. "Thanks for encouraging me to get rid of that excess baggage, partner. I can serve the Lord much more effectively now."

"That's for sure," I said, "the lighter, the better. I've learned that pioneers need to travel light. You may have to come back here from time to time to get rid of stuff you've picked up on the journey. **It's a shame how easily we get encumbered by things that don't really matter.** I guess you've realized by now why my stack of baggage is so big.

"One thing for sure," I said confidently, "anything the Lord wants us to carry is light and manageable. It won't weigh us down and burden us to the point of ineffectiveness. When we follow the Commander-in-Chief's orders we can easily shoulder the load! He gives us abundant grace."[1]

SPLASH!

"Shhh! Listen," I said, stopping in my tracks on the boardwalk in front of the windowless silo. "Did you hear that?"

We stood perfectly still, listening for the slightest sound from inside the secret room. "It sounds like someone moving clay pots around," Tim whispered.

A creaking noise, like a door opening, drifted toward us. "I think it's the beam above the well," I said.

The circular timber revolved above the opening and the rope uncoiled into The Well of His Presence. Something splashed deep within its sacred depths; instantly a prophetic anticipation seized us. Tim and I glanced at each other in confirming agreement.

"Another spiritual pioneer has discovered The Secret Place," I said, with a sense of satisfaction. "It's happening, Tim. Thank God!"

EVIL DAYS

We moved on past the General's Store. Just as he did every day, Paul was inside sorting the mail and waiting expectantly for pioneers to come by and pick it up. He waved at us. We tipped our hats and smiled gratefully.

As we passed the school house, I felt a keen sense of urgency. I knew time was running out on God's clock. "Judgment is coming!" I warned, glancing away from Main Street across the open prairie.

"One thing's certain," I said, turning my head back in Tim's direction. "These are perilous days. Self love abounds. Everyone is greedy for more money. People go around boasting about their knowledge and success. In their arrogance and pride they think nothing of blaspheming God." [2]

"I heard enough cursing and swearing last night to last a lifetime," he responded. "People love pleasure more than they love God."

"We really have our work cut out for us," I said. "We've got to take back what the devil has stolen. We must walk carefully. It's time to put away foolish things and seek the Lord's wisdom and discernment. We've got to make the best of our time. These days are evil!" [3]

Man's wisdom will never get the job done.

WARFARE STRATEGY

"We must come to The Secret Place often," I urged. "Man's wisdom will never get the job done. Only an understanding of the will of the Lord can suffice! End-time warfare strategies come from communion with the Almighty. I know that for certain," I said. "I've been to the strategy room of heaven."

Tim looked at me in amazement. "You have?" he gulped. "What's it like? Tell me!"

"Some day, when we get some time," I replied, "I'll show you my journal. It's all written there." [4]

"I can't wait! That's really incredible!"

"I know!" I said, humbly. "It's an incredible place! You'll be amazed!"

LISTEN UP!

We darted past the partially painted building and rushed into the *Koinonia* Café. The usual morning crowd had gathered for fresh food. I noticed a few new faces among the familiar ones. Amid shouts of friendly greeting I made my way to the back of the room and climbed up onto the counter.

"Listen up, everyone," I yelled, to get everybody's attention. The room fell silent. All eyes were on me.

"I've got to tell you what Tim and I discovered down the street last night next to the bunkhouse where we've been sleeping. You know where I mean, the saloon?"

"Yeah, we know," someone shouted from across the room.

Another pioneer waved his cup, spilling coffee onto the floor. "I don't go in there," he bragged arrogantly. "Not a good crowd!"

"Watch it, that's hot," a woman nearby retorted, wiping the black spots on her dress.

"It's really not a saloon," I shouted back. "It's a jail! And there are a great number of prisoners locked up inside."

A murmur of surprise spread through the assembled crowd. Some were confused. Others had a sudden look of disdain. It was a mixed response for sure.

PLANNING THE RESCUE

"We led several people to Jesus last night," I continued.

Tim butted in, "There's an incredible harvest of souls in there, folks. They desperately need our help. We're going back today!"

Suddenly the tone of the group changed. Everyone seemed excited at the prospect and challenge of the work ahead. They gathered in clusters around the tables discussing plans to invade the jailhouse. It wasn't long till some burly believers started pounding their Bibles on the tables in judgment. A few harsh pioneers began to stir up anger among the warriors.

"Wait," I shouted, "there's more! You need something first." I reached into my shepherd's bag and held the milk glass container up high for everyone to see.

"Please don't go running up the street until you apply this salve to your eyes. If you do, someone may get hurt! Believe me, I know. I had to learn the hard way."

I handed the jar of ointment to Tim. **He moved back and forth among the crowd, offering them the salve. Each warrior took a little of the balm and**

applied it gently to his or her eyes. The Bible thumping stopped, and before long tears of intercession broke out all over the room. Men, women and children were weeping as they prayed fervently for those in prison up the street. Minutes turned into hours as the Holy Spirit interceded through the pioneers assembled at the *Koinonia* Café. No one left the room.

A WARRIOR'S MEAL

It was late morning before the heavy anointing for intercession lifted and people began to talk about the work ahead.

"Before we go," I said, "let's break bread together."

A single large loaf was produced from the kitchen. We all bowed to give thanks.

"This is Your body, Lord, broken for us!" I prayed. "Let us be Your Body today, Your army commissioned and sent out to heal the sick and set the captives free. Anoint us to be Your soldiers of compassion."[5] I broke the loaf and passed the pieces among the warriors.

One of the pioneers handed me a clay goblet from behind the counter. It was plain, light brown and had a sandy, grainy feel on the outside. It was filled with wine. I lifted the goblet toward my fellow soldiers. "The cup of the New Covenant," I shouted with a surge of emotion. "We bless it!"

> *Let us be Your Body today, Your army commissioned and sent out to heal the sick and set the captives free.*

Everyone stood to their feet. They held their individual cups up toward the single vessel extended above my head. Everyone shouted in unison, "The cup of blessing which we bless!" [6]

The shout rumbled down the street of Frontier Town like an avalanche and cascaded into the Town Jail. "What's that noise?" someone imprisoned within the walls of the saloon said. "I thought I heard someone shouting from up the street!"

"I'm not sure," another patron replied, "Sounded to me like something about a blessing and a cup!"

"Oh, it's nothing," the barmaid said, and they went back to their numbing activities. They didn't realize that the entire town was about to overrun their space. They didn't have a clue who was about to invade their territory!

I tipped the goblet to drink from the clay vessel. To my surprise, the interior of the plain goblet was made of pure silver. The rich red liquid it contained tinted the interior surface blood red. "It's Jesus' cup," I confessed, and drank deeply.[7] I passed the cup to Timothy. He drank from it and then passed it through the café until all had tasted its contents.

I'LL CATCH UP WITH YOU LATER

"Go, in Jesus' name!" I said, breaking the reverent silence. "The harvest is waiting."

Groups of two or three banded together in agreement and left the *Koinonia* Café headed down the street of Frontier Town toward the jailhouse.

"Come on, Tim," I said, "let's join the laborers."

We strolled out of the door. Just as we turned toward the saloon at the far end of Main Street, I heard a familiar neighing. I spun around in delight; there stood Spirit Wind calmly waiting by the hitching post at the opposite end of the street. Gillar and Mannor stood at ease beside him.

"Go ahead, Timothy," I encouraged, "I'll catch up with you later! If somehow we get separated, meet me tonight at The Secret Place."

"All right partner," he said, and sauntered off alone down the wood sidewalk whistling a happy tune of praise. **My last view of Tim was when he stopped abruptly on the deck and disappeared into the unfinished, half painted house next to the café.**

FINAL DETAILS

I made my way up the street toward Spirit Wind, past the café and Jacob's Pottery Shop. I was surprised to see my own clay vessel sitting in the doorway cooling in the morning shade. Jacob smiled and waved.

"Almost finished now," he said. "I can tell by its sound!" He nodded a goodbye and went back to the vessel he was shaping on the wheel.

When I reached Abraham's place, he was standing in the doorway. "Come on in, I've been expecting you," he said, motioning toward the registration table. "We need to take care of final details."

I glanced over at the schedule hanging beside the entrance of the log cabin. My name had been moved from the "Arriving" column and shifted to the one that said "Departing." A different configuration of stars appeared after it to indicate the elapsed spiritual time. It made me think of the stars my grade school teachers used to put on my homework assignments when they were done well.

"What's going on?" I said, as I approached the registration table.

"Take this with you, son. Your time here is over," Abraham said, setting a document on top of the counter.

I looked in disbelief. "So soon? There must be more to learn. I'm not ready yet." I lifted the paper and held it up to the light. I read it with mixed emotions.

"Now the Lord had said to Abram: 'Get out of your country, from your family and from your father's house, to a land that I will show you. I will make you a great nation; I will bless you and make your name great; and you shall be a blessing. I will bless those who bless you, and I will curse him who curses you; and in you all the families of the earth shall be blessed'" (Genesis 12:1-3).

Certificate of Completion

In Recognition of Obedient Response to the Call of God

This is to certify that

Dale Arthur Fife

has successfully completed the primary course of instruction

for Spiritual Pioneers and is hereby

accorded the affirmation of his peers

and mentors and fully commissioned to possess the Land.

Signed on this day of our Lord , September 24th At Frontier Town;

Abraham, the Journeyer   *Jacob, the Potter's Assistant*

Paul, the Pioneer   *Jesus, the Son*

"Now the Lord had said to Abram,

'Get out of your country, from your family and from your father's house, to a land that I will show you.'"

"Going on Still" (Genesis 12:9)

I looked at Abraham with a quizzical expression. "Going on still?" I asked.

"Yes," he replied reassuringly. "Going on still."

"I'd better be going then," I affirmed.

JUST THE BEGINNING

Jesus stood outside the door waiting for me. "You have done well, son," He said. "I am proud of you! Spirit Wind will take you on from here; but wait, let Me have your diploma. I'll keep it in a safe place for you." I handed Him my diploma with a sense of inadequacy.

"This is just the beginning," He said taking it from my hands. "You have passed this test! I can trust you to teach others. But your training must continue elsewhere. I'll meet you in The Secret Place again soon."

Jesus turned and walked to the end of Main Street and onto the construction site. I descended the stairs to the street to greet Spirit Wind. Mannor and Gillar assisted me up into the saddle, obviously glad to see me because several days had gone by since our last encounter.

Spirit Wind lifted his majestic head and tossed his white mane in the air. With an energizing whinny, he turned toward the open plain and trotted out of town.

As we passed the construction site, I was astounded at the progress on the house. **The walls and roof were in place; through the window I could see Jesus hanging my diploma on the wall.**

Frontier Town gradually blended into the horizon behind us and became a vivid memory, a prophetic vision recorded on the pages of my journal, a place of great spiritual significance for all of God's servants.

With conclusive surging energy, Spirit Wind rose to a steady gallop and headed for The Well of His Presence.

Chapter Twenty-Three

GET YE UP!

Malchior[1] deliberately positioned the clay water pot directly at his feet so he could see into it. His presence gave a guarded importance to the vessel.

"I'm glad he's here to help us," Mannor said to Gillar, in gratitude for Malchior's presence.

"Yes," Gillar replied. "It's good to have someone share the responsibility of guarding all these vessels."

Angels on Assignment

I watched the two angels move around The Well of God's Presence with an airy lightness. Mannor stopped to adjust the location of a tall, urn-shaped vase that had a delicate feminine form to it.

One of God's prophetesses, no doubt, I thought. *There is such an incredible variety of pottery here at the well. An entire lifespan would not provide sufficient time just to examine a few of these revealed mysteries and secrets.*

Gillar smiled at me as he passed by at the perimeter of the assembled vessels. "It has begun," he said, and walked directly toward the chest containing the golden writing instruments.

"It has begun?" I called after him. "What's begun?"

He didn't reply. Instead, he held his finger up and frowned. The simple gesture made me realize that I shouldn't interrupt him. He needed to concentrate on the task at hand. I would soon find out what he meant.

183

SPIRIT WIND

The wooden chest sat exactly where I had first seen it before my angelic companions escorted me to Frontier Town. Gillar waited in front of the box for two additional angels to appear and then lifted the lid to expose the pens. **The three celestial friends stood before the open box admiring the writing instruments with a reverence that clearly communicated the sacredness of their assignment.**

Gillar reached into the box and grasped one of the cylinders. His hand and forearm glistened from the radiance of its luster. When he closed the protective lid it sealed with a solid bang, like someone dropping a piano keyboard cover.

IT HAS BEGUN

"Guard it well, Samshiel![2] It is a special revelation from The Well of His Presence for this new generation," Gillar said, as he handed the magnificently crafted pen to the angel next to him.

Mannor looked up from his kneeling position amidst the vessels where he was dusting a particularly large urn. "When you arrive, please do me a favor, my friend," he said.

"What is it?" B'Azeliel[3], the second angel, replied.

"When you see Spirit Wind, greet him for me. You never know where he will show up. He's like the wind – you don't know where he comes from or where he is going, but you definitely know when he's around."[4]

"I will," B'Azeliel promised. "I'm certain we will encounter him on our journey into the well."

Samshiel and B'Azeliel turned to enter The Well of His Presence. The golden pen they carried sent sparkling flashes of light over the pure surface of the water. A vessel near the stone wall of the well captured the reflections, a prophetic precursor to the fullness of the new revelation. Just as suddenly as they appeared, the two angels were gone into the Lord's presence to escort one more end-time warrior on another prophetic journey of revelation.

"I wonder who it is," I said, looking at Gillar, with fond thoughts of Timothy racing through my mind. "There are so many people already in Frontier Town. Perhaps the scroll is for one of them?

"Maybe the Lord is summoning another end-time warrior into His presence in the Strategy Room of Heaven or sending another apostle or prophet to build the Church. It might even be a teacher! He knows how desperately we need anointed teachers with the Forest of Deception growing larger every day.[5] Why, if it were not for His mercy and grace, even the elect would be deceived."

TELL THIS GENERATION!

Malchior bent over the plain clay pot he was guarding and stirred the clear water with his fingers.

"That looks familiar," I said, intrigued by its recognizable shape. Then it dawned on me. The vessel was identical to the one I had seen cooling in the shade at Jacob's Pottery Shop just before I left Frontier Town.

"That looks just like my vessel, Malchior!" I shouted, in surprise. My memory clicked into gear. Scenes from inside the potter's shop on Main Street appeared before me like slides flashing on a screen.

"The Master Potter does perfect work," I said, watching my life scroll past. My thoughts gradually subsided like the ripples on the surface of the water inside the vessel, steadily dissipating to a placid smoothness.

Malchior stood to his feet and spoke with confident boldness. "You have been commissioned by the Lord of the harvest to carry the message in this vessel to this generation. Go through the church! Tell God's house to prepare and make ready their provisions. We will soon break camp. It is the hour of crossing over. **The time has come to possess the end of the age! Be strong and of good courage! The Lord is with you.**[6]

"Tell God's warriors that every place they put their feet to possess it in the name of Jesus, He will give it to them. Disease and sickness will be healed; the prisoners will be set free. This generation is called to be a new breed, a mountain-moving force![7] This is the Joshua generation.

"Remind them of the spiritual combination of faith, hope and love. It will open doors that oppose them," Malchior continued. "Advise them to travel light. The Almighty will provide storehouses of mercy on the way."

"And one last thing before you go," he cautioned. "This is very important, friend of God! Don't forget to refer often to your *Field Manual for Spiritual Pioneers*! It's designed for use in the world. It will withstand the rigors of spiritual warfare. If at any time you need to return to Frontier Town, open your manual and locate the appropriate place in the text. The Holy Spirit will take you there and provide the instruction and wisdom you need."

GUARDIANS

Gillar and Mannor left their labor among the vessels. "Come, friend of God! We will walk with you up the path that leads from the well," Mannor said. [8]

We climbed the sloping path to the roadway of life in the distance. When I glanced back to say goodbye, Malchior was gone and the full vessel he was guarding sat next to the well.

The sweet atmosphere at The Well of His Presence dissipated with each step up the hillside. The trees and underbrush thickened and the path narrowed as we approached the busy highway. Gillar and Mannor walked so close to me that they kept bumping me. "Sorry," Gillar said, rubbing against my shoulder.

"I don't mind," I quickly replied. "Having you nearby encourages me. I feel protected and guarded."

When we finally neared the hidden entrance to The Secret Place, I reached down to be sure that I still had my shepherd's bag with me. I quickly took stock.

"Let's see," I reassured myself. "The eye salve, the cup, the parchment, the Field Manual for Spiritual Pioneers. Yep, they're all here safely inside." I felt a growing excitement and anticipation building within my spirit. I couldn't wait to get back onto the busy road.

ON THE ROAD AGAIN!

Gillar and Mannor were shocked. Totally unlike my first exit from The Secret Place, I didn't hesitate for a second. I burst out of the bushes onto the busy roadway filled with people rushing to and fro and stood right in the middle of the street searching the faces of each person who hurried by.

Every now and then I felt someone touch me, but no one was close enough. I smiled, realizing that it was Gillar or Mannor. The people passing by couldn't see my angelic companions, but I knew they were beside me, right here in the midst of civilization.

A young lady approached with a cheerful expression on her face. **She was humming a tune that I immediately recognized. My spirit leapt within me.**

"Why, it's the same tune Timothy was whistling when we parted back in Frontier Town." I said in astonishment. I hesitated as she walked right past me, but I couldn't contain myself any longer. "Ma'am!" I shouted. "Excuse me, ma'am. Good day to you."

She stopped and turned to me with a warm smile. "Good morning to you, sir. What a gorgeous day it is."

"I apologize for my boldness, but I couldn't help notice that tune you were humming just now. I've heard it before. Do you mind telling me where you learned it?"

"Why, not at all," she happily replied. "It's one of my favorite choruses. We sing it at our church all the time."

My face lit up with excitement. "You're a Christian?" I half asked, half declared. "You must be a Christian!"

"Yes!" she replied. "I met Jesus a few weeks ago. My life has been completely turned around. I'm on my way to my home just around the bend about a mile from here. I'm almost there."

She jerked her head around with a perky joyfulness and looked longingly down the road to the turn in the distance. A tear graced her eye. "I can't wait to get there. I've been gone for months. I miss my Mom and Dad so much."

A familiar tinkling sound caught my attention as her silver earring danced against her neck. Her brownish-black hair had grown longer and her deep black eyes were so full of joy and life.

"We've met before!" I blurted out in astonishment.

"We have?" she replied, quizzically. "I don't recall meeting you. The places I've been in the past six months are not likely to be frequented by someone as nice as you!"

"You might be surprised," I responded. "I'm learning that God leads his warriors to where the battle is!"

"Well, I'm sorry, but I really must be going. I'm so eager to get home!" she said.

HERE'S A GIFT FOR YOU.

"Wait a minute," I insisted. "Let me give you something that will help you in the days ahead." I quickly loosened the drawstring and reached into my shepherd's bag for my field manual. "Here," I said, "Take this and read it. I think it will come in very handy!" I surprised myself by my willingness to part so easily with the valuable volume that Malchior had told me to use often. "But," I said under my breath, "she really needs it, Lord!"

She grasped the canvas covered book with delight. "Oh, how wonderful of you!" she replied. "I shall cherish this and read it as soon as I get home."

"Oh, by the way, my card is stuck inside one of the pages. If you ever want to talk with me or need some help, please give me a call."

"I will!" she replied. "I certainly will!" and with those final words she turned and walked on, happily humming her tune.

THE HIDDEN ENTRANCE

I watched her open the book and leaf through the pages as she sped away. She paused momentarily to read my card. "Dale Arthur Fife – Spiritual Pioneer, Searching for a city whose builder and maker is God. To Conquer, To Love, To Redeem." She turned and gave a grateful wave of acknowledgment.

I motioned with all the enthusiasm I could muster, pointing excitedly toward the hidden entrance next to me at the side of the road. "The Secret Place," I shouted, but she was too far away to hear my voice above the din and clatter of bustling traffic. She nodded with a puzzled look, and then turned toward home and disappeared around the bend.

I reached down to secure the drawstring on my shepherd's bag. "What's this?" I gasped with absolute joy. I could feel the familiar square shape of my field manual inside. "It's here," I said incredulously. To my amazement, my *Field Manual for Spiritual Pioneers* was still in the bag.

"But how, Lord?" I said. Then I remembered! "Things aren't what they seem to be in Frontier Town!"

The vision ended.

ACKNOWLEDGEMENTS

Books are not written in a vacuum. There are so many to thank. First of all, my life is so blessed because of you, Eunice. You are my best friend. We share the same passion for His presence. Your prayers, encouragement and unselfish love have made this journey a joy. The eagerness on your face, the sparkle in your eyes and the delight of sharing each day with me as the Lord revealed Frontier Town to us is forever written upon my heart. We journey on together. I love you! Thanks, babe.

Heartfelt thanks to my secretary, Damaris Prendergast. You dared to face the challenge of taking my personal journal and deciphering my sometimes illegible writing into readable words on a computer screen. You saved me hours of work.

A hundred words of appreciation would not be enough to thank Trudy Haight for poring over the manuscript for days, editing until her eyes were bloodshot. You are a gift from God! Thank you so much for bringing this book up to a standard of excellence pleasing to Him.

To the many intercessors who held me up before the throne of grace, especially Daniel and Janet Fife, Lorrie and Brian Fife, Carol Missik, Jill Mitchell, Briskilla Zananiri, Jamie LaFond, Weston and Karen Brooks, Barbara and Gerry LaChance, Ian and Michelle Gunn, Jim and Jan Erb, and all the prayer warriors from the Potter's House in Farmington, The River of Life in Tolland, and Covenant Church of Pittsburgh: Thank you so much! May God's favor and blessing be multiplied to you a hundredfold.

Over the past few years I have received a host of letters and emails from readers whose lives have been touched, blessed and changed by *The Secret Place* and *The Hidden Kingdom.* My prayer is that your lives will be further blessed by this third volume drawn from deep in The Well of His Presence.

Jesus! You are the reason I live. Intimacy with You is the passion of my life. If I can tell just one person how much You love them and how You long for intimacy with them, I will be satisfied. Use this scroll for Your Kingdom purposes. I honor You above all!

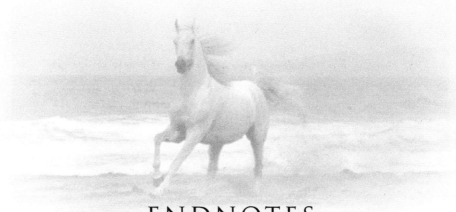

ENDNOTES

INTRODUCTION

1. Roger Green and Walter Hooper, *C.S. Lewis, A Biography* (NY: Harcourt Brace & Company, Harvest Edition, 1994), 169.

2. Billy Graham, *Angels, God's Secret Agents* (NY: Doubleday, 1975), 24.

3. See Leonard Sweet, *Out of the Question, Into the Mystery* (Colorado Springs: Random House, Waterbrook Press, 2004), 194-195.

4. C.S. Lewis, *Perelandra* (NY: Scribner, 1996), 40.

CHAPTER ONE: THE PROPHETIC SCRIBE

1. W. E. Vine, *Vine's Complete Expository Dictionary of Old and New Testament Words* (Nashville: Thomas Nelson, 1996), 190.

2. See Acts 2:14-21.

3. For a complete description of the vision of The Well of His Presence see Dr. Dale A. Fife, *The Secret Place, Passionately Pursuing His Presence* (New Kensington, PA: Whitaker House, 2001), 104, 112.

4. These two angels first appeared when I received the vision written in my first book, *The Secret Place*. I did not learn their names until much later.

   My educated guess is that the name, Gillar, means *hero, one who knows the regions and valleys of vision*. It is derived from *Gehazi*, valley of vision; *Geliloth*, regions; and *Gibbar*, hero. See the *Scofield Reference Bible* (NY: Oxford Press, 1945), *Dictionary of Proper Names*, 19.

   Mannor means *habitation of rest*. It is derived from, *Manoah*, rest; and *Maon*, habitation. (*Scofield Reference Bible* (NY: Oxford Press, 1945), 32.

5. Fife, *The Secret Place*, 51, 61.

6. Ibid., 161, 162.

CHAPTER TWO: DEEPER IN THE WELL

1. *"The secret things belong to the Lord our God, but those things which are revealed belong to us and to our children forever, that we may do all the words of this law"* (Deuteronomy 29:29).

"Ask, and it will be given to you; seek, and you will find; knock, and it will be opened to you. For everyone who asks receives, and he who seeks finds, and to him who knocks it will be opened." (Matthew 7:7-8).

2. See Dr. Dale A. Fife, *The Secret Place, Passionately Pursuing His Presence* (New Kensington, PA: Whitaker House, 2001), *The Roadway of Life*, 223.

3. See Dr. Dale A. Fife, *The Hidden Kingdom, Journey into the Heart of God* (New Kensington, PA: Whitaker House, 2003), 67.

4. Ibid., 81.

5. *Let no one deceive himself. If anyone among you seems to be wise in this age, let him become a fool that he may become wise. For the wisdom of this world is foolishness with God. For it is written, 'He catches the wise in their own craftiness'; and again, 'The Lord knows the thoughts of the wise, that they are futile.' Therefore let no one boast in men. For all things are yours...* (First Corinthians 3: 18-21; see also Matthew 13: 10-17)

CHAPTER THREE: FRONTIER TOWN

1. See Dr. Dale A. Fife, *The Secret Place, Passionately Pursuing His Presence* (New Kensington, PA: Whitaker House, 2001), 104.

2. See Matthew 8: 5-13.

3. Fife, *The Secret Place*, 187-200.

   During my journey into the strategy room of heaven I saw a door located to the right of the podium on the far side of the room. It was directly opposite the one leading into the Throne Room. Even though I was aware of it, I did not sense the Lord's permission to go there. I believe it leads to God's library: a collection of information in every imaginable form, as well as forms yet unknown to man. The deep things of God are catalogued there. We already know that some of these books exist and are mentioned in the Bible. Although I would have delighted in spending hours in God's library, I realized that the purpose for which the Lord had summoned me into His presence was urgent, and did not allow for time to browse the contents of this incredible depository of God's collected volumes of endless wisdom, knowledge and mystery.

4. *"In the beginning was the Word, and the Word was with God, and the Word was God"* (John 1:1).

CHAPTER FOUR: MAIN STREET

1. Bishop Joseph Garlington, Sunday morning message at Covenant Church of Pittsburgh, November 2004. See Isaiah 26:3-ff.

2. See Zachariah 4:6.

CHAPTER FIVE: SPIRIT WIND

1. Dr. Dale A. Fife, *The Secret Place, Passionately Pursuing His Presence* (New Kensington, PA: Whitaker House, 2001), 125-128.

2. Suggested Reading: Laurie Beth Jones, *Jesus in Blue Jeans: A Practical Guide to Everyday Spirituality* (New York: Hyperion, 1997).

3. See Isaiah 55:8.

4. See Matthew 20:16.

5.   See First Samuel 16.

6.   See First Corinthians 8:1-2.

7.   See First Corinthians 1:18-31.

8.   See Matthew 20:20-28.

9.   See James 4:6; First Peter 5:5; Luke 11:43; Matthew 14:7-11.

10. See Acts 9:1-19.

11. See Matthew 20:16; John 15:16; Romans 8:28.

CHAPTER SIX: THE CONSTRUCTION SITE

1.   See Dr. Dale A. Fife, *The Hidden Kingdom, Journey into the Heart of God* (New Kensington, PA: Whitaker House, 2003), 134-135, 141-142, 188-189, 203-204, 239.

2.   Ibid., 141-144.

3.   See Hebrews 6:1-3.

4.   See Hebrews 6:1-2.

5.   See Ephesians 4:11.

CHAPTER EIGHT: HOME, SWEET HOME

1.   See Song of Solomon 1:2.

2.   See Dr. Dale A. Fife, *The Hidden Kingdom, Journey into the Heart of God* (New Kensington, PA: Whitaker House, 2003), 240-241.

CHAPTER NINE: THE DOORWAY TO DESTINY

1.   See Dr. Dale A. Fife, *The Hidden Kingdom, Journey into the Heart of God* (New Kensington, PA: Whitaker House, 2003), 77-81.

2.   *"When the morning stars sang together, and all the sons of God shouted for joy..."* (Job 38:7)

3.   See Isaiah 55:8.

4.   See Exodus 21:1-5; Deuteronomy 15:12-18.

5.   See Hebrews 11.

CHAPTER TEN: KINGDOM CREATIONS

1.   See Dr. Dale A. Fife, *The Secret Place, Passionately Pursuing His Presence* (New Kensington, PA: Whitaker House, 2001), 200.

2.   See Dr. Dale A. Fife, *The Hidden Kingdom, Journey into the Heart of God* (New Kensington, PA: Whitaker House, 2003).

3.   See Genesis 13:1-18; Hebrews 6:1-3.

4.   See Ecclesiastes 12:9-11.

CHAPTER ELEVEN: THE POTTER'S HANDS

1.   The Greek word for criticism is *sarx*. It literally means, "to cut to the flesh." We derive our contemporary word "sarcasm" from it.

2. See Genesis 32:28.

3. See Isaiah 64:8.

4. See Hebrews 13:17.

CHAPTER TWELVE: *KOINONIA* CAFÉ

1. See Dr. Dale A. Fife, *The Hidden Kingdom, Journey into the Heart of God* (New Kensington, PA: Whitaker House, 2003), 87.

2. See Mark 6:7.

3. See Acts 16:3.

CHAPTER THIRTEEN: UNIVERSE-CITY

1. The sun actually stood still for an entire day. See Joshua 10:1-15.

   "So the sun stood still, and the moon stopped, till the people had revenge upon their enemies. ...and there has been no day like that, before it or after it, that the Lord heeded the voice of a man; for the Lord fought for Israel" (Joshua 10:13-14).

2. See Matthew 2:13-23.

3. See Second Corinthians 1:12.

4. See Proverbs 4:7.

5. See Proverbs 16:16.

6. See Proverbs 19: 8.

7. See James 1:2-8.

8. See Colossians 2:9-10.

CHAPTER FIFTEEN: OVERCOMING YOUR FEARS

1. See Matthew 17:20.

2. See Philippians 3:12-14.

3. See Matthew 26:31-35.

4. Origen, the great historian, reports that Peter was crucified head downwards. "When he was brought to the cross he made the request, 'Not with my head up. My Master died that way! Crucify me head downward. I die for my Lord but I am not worthy to die like Him.'" Herbert Lockyer, *All the Apostles of the Bible* (Grand Rapids, Michigan: Zondervan, 1972), 257.

5. *"The heart is deceitful above all things, and desperately wicked; who can know it? I, the Lord, search the heart, I test the mind, even to give every man according to his ways, according to the fruit of his doings"* (Jeremiah 17:9-10).

6. See Second Corinthians 12:9; Romans 8:26.

7. See Philippians 4:13.

8. See Matthew 18:19.

CHAPTER SEVENTEEN: THE POST OFFICE

1. See First Samuel 18:7.

2.   See Dr. Dale A. Fife, *The Secret Place, Passionately Pursuing His Presence* (New Kensington, PA: Whitaker House, 2001), 176.

CHAPTER EIGHTEEN: END TIME WARRIORS

1.   See James 4:1-10.

2.   See Romans 8:26-27.

3.   See First Timothy 1:18; Ephesians 6:10-20.

CHAPTER NINETEEN: TRAVELING LIGHT

1.   See First Peter 4:8.

CHAPTER TWENTY: THE SALOON

1.   See Galatians 5:19-21.

2.   See Romans 1:18-32.

3.   See Ephesians 4:26; 6:10-17.

4.   See Matthew 26:51-56.

5.   See John 8:7.

6   See Dr. Dale A. Fife, *The Hidden Kingdom, Journey into the Heart of God* (New Kensington, PA: Whitaker House, 2003), 71-76.

7.   See Romans 12:21.

CHAPTER TWENTY-ONE: COMPASSION ON MAIN STREET

1.   See Romans 8:28.

2.   See Lamentations 3:22; Psalm 78:38, 86:15.

3.   See Matthew 9:36, 18:33; Mark 1:41, 8:2; Luke 7:13.

4.   See Matthew 14:14.

5.   Cf. Mark 1:41; Luke. 7:13.

6.   See John 11:33, 35.

7.   See Revelation 3:18.

8.   See First Corinthians 10:13.

9.   See John 3:16.

10. See Romans 6:23.

11. See Second Corinthians 5:17.

12. See Eugene Peterson, *The Message* (Colorado Springs: Navpress, *2002)*, Hebrews 4:12-13.

13. The word *compassion* has several shades of meaning in the New Testament. When used as a verb, it describes an action motivated by pity and feelings of distress. It is accompanied by deep yearning and longing due to the suffering of others. In fact, it means, "to suffer with someone else," affected by their anguish and desperation. *Compassion* requires the response of mercy and kindness. It moves us to do something to assist those in need. It was the compelling suffering of mankind that moved Christ to action.

When used as a noun, compassion describes the heart of mercy, or someone with "bowels of compassion." It is a visceral, gut-wrenching, heart-rending emotion that cries out for mercy.

W. E. Vine, *Expository Dictionary of New Testament Words* (New Jersey: Fleming, Revell Company, 1966), 218-219.

CHAPTER TWENTY-TWO: FORMING THE POSSE

1. See First Peter 5:7; Matthew 11:28-30; Philippians 4:6.

2. See Second Timothy 3:1-5.

3. See Romans 12:9, 17, 21; Genesis 3:5, 6:5; Matthew 6:13; Ephesians 5:15-17; First Timothy 6:10.

4. See Dr. Dale A. Fife, *The Secret Place, Passionately Pursuing His Presence* (New Kensington, PA: Whitaker House, 2001), 187-189.

5. See Matthew 28:18-20; Acts 1:8.

6. See Matthew 25:26-28; First Corinthians 10:14-17.

7. See Dr. Dale A. Fife, *The Hidden Kingdom, Journey into the Heart of God* (New Kensington, PA: Whitaker House, 2003), 87-96.

   Compare: Matthew 20:20-23, 26:27; Luke 22:20; First Corinthians 11:25.

CHAPTER TWENTY-THREE: GET YE UP!

1. *Malchior* means "Jehovah's king," derived from *Malchiah*.

   (See *The Scofield Reference Bible* (NY: Oxford University Press, 1945, Dictionary of Proper Names), 31.

2. *Samshiel* means "One whom God hears," derived from *Samuel*, "heard of God"; *Sheal*, "prayer." Ezra 10:29; *Shealtiel*, "I asked God," Ezra 3:2.

   (See *The Scofield Reference Bible* (NY: Oxford University Press, 1945, Dictionary of Proper Names), 40, 42.

3. *B'Azeliel* means "noble one, whom God strengthens." Derived from *Azarae*, "whom God helps"; and *Bezaleel*, "in the shadow of God."

   (See *The Scofield Reference Bible* (NY: Oxford University Press, 1945, Dictionary of Proper Names), 8, 11.

4. See John 3:8.

5. See Dr. Dale A. Fife, *The Secret Place, Passionately Pursuing His Presence* (New Kensington, PA: Whitaker House, 2001), 139ff.

6. See Joshua 1:6-11.

7. See Joshua 1:3; John 11:22; Matthew 17:20-21.

8. Fife, *The Secret Place*, 223-225.

ABOUT THE AUTHOR

D r. Dale Arthur Fife is a gifted pastor, author, teacher and musician with an insatiable passion for intimacy with God. His zeal for the Lord has led him on an incredible journey from his first pastorate of a small rural church in a coalmining town outside of Johnstown, PA, to the co-founding of a large, multiracial, inner-city church in Pittsburgh. After four decades of experience in a variety of ministry settings, he now provides apostolic counsel to several churches, ministries and individuals. His best selling books, *The Secret Place, Passionately Pursuing God's Presence* and The *Hidden Kingdom, Journey Into the Heart of God*, have blessed and encouraged thousands to seek a closer walk with Jesus.

As a worship leader at the first outdoor Jesus Festivals in the mid seventies, or in his present ministry pastoring and speaking at churches, conferences and men's and women's gatherings for leaders or intercessors worldwide, Dale's enthusiasm and hunger for God is contagious. His wisdom, maturity and genuine spiritual concern for others have caused many to regard him as a spiritual father in the Lord. His insightful teaching has inspired and blessed many of God's people around the world.

Dale graduated Summa Cum Laude from the University of Pittsburgh and completed seminary studies at Boston University School of Theology. He continued to pursue graduate studies at Pittsburgh Theological Seminary. The Doctor of Divinity degree was conferred upon him by New Life College in Bangalore, India.

Dale and Eunice were married in 1963 and have two sons, Scott and Brian, and six grandchildren, Brandon, Aaron, Brianne, Anthony, Joanna and Asa. They live in Bradenton, Florida where they co-pastor a thriving church. They have also established Mountain Top Global Ministries, a network of ministries, leaders and pastors with local, regional and international impact. Dale and Eunice travel together throughout the world proclaiming the good news of God's Kingdom and encouraging the body of Christ to passionately pursue God's presence.

Dr. Fife is available for speaking engagements upon request. He can be reached at MnTopMin@aol.com. You can also log on to Dr. Fife's web site at www.TPHCT.com. for information regarding additional resources or itinerary.

Spirit Wind

Along with the author's best selling books,

 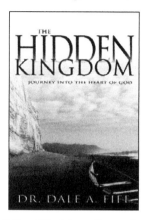

The Secret Place   and   *The Hidden Kingdom*

may be ordered online at:
www.tphct.com
The Potter's House Church
860-677-1850

And are also available at your local Christian bookstore or bookseller.

Visit the website resource page to check out the many teaching CD's
and DVD's available through Dr. Fife's ministry.

Dr. Fife is available for speaking engagements. To schedule him for
your church, conference or event, email or phone:

Dr. Dale A. Fife
Mountain Top Global Ministries
724-946-2725 / 860-836-1247
MnTopMin@aol.com